THE SOULS OF WHITE FOLK

THE SOULS OF WHITE FOLK

*African American Writers
Theorize Whiteness*

Veronica T. Watson

University Press of Mississippi / Jackson

Margaret Walker Alexander Series
in African American Studies

www.upress.state.ms.us

The University Press of Mississippi is a member
of the Association of American University Presses.

Parts of Chapter 2, "Shaping herself into a dutiful wife":
Demythologizing White Femininity and the White Home in Frank Yerby's
The Foxes of Harrow and Zora Neale Hurston's *Seraph on the Suwanee*" were
first published as "Demythologizing Whiteness in Frank Yerby's *The Foxes
of Harrow*," *Journal of Ethnic American Literature* 1 (2011): 92–110.

First printing 2013
∞
Library of Congress Cataloging-in-Publication Data

Watson, Veronica T.
The souls of white folk : African American writers theorize whiteness / Veronica T. Watson.
pages cm — (Margaret Walker Alexander series in African American studies)
Includes bibliographical references and index.
ISBN 978-1-61703-889-1 (cloth : alk. paper) — ISBN 978-1-61703-890-7 (ebook)
1. American literature—African American authors—History and criticism.
2. American literature—19th century—History and criticism.
3. American literature—19th century—History and criticism.
4. Whites—Race identity—In literature. 5. Whites in literature. I. Title.
PS153.N5W355 2013
810.9'896073—dc23   2013006402

British Library Cataloging-in-Publication Data available

First I give praise to God.
This journey has deepened my faith.
And to Herb Sr., Herb Jr., and Zora,
All my love. Always.

Epigraph credits

James Baldwin
Excerpted from "The Nigger We Invent" © 1969 by James Baldwin. Colleted in *The Cross of Redemption*, published by Pantheon Books. Reprinted by arrangement with the James Baldwin Estate. Excerpted from "The White Problem © 1964 by James Baldwin. Originally published in *100 Years of Emancipation*. Collected in *The Cross of Redemption*, published by Pantheon Books. Reprinted by arrangement with the James Baldwin Estate. Excerpted from "Letter to My Nephew," © by James Baldwin. Originally published in *The Progressive*. Collected in *The Fire Next Time*, published by Vintage Books. Reprinted by arrangment with the James Baldwin Estate.

Barbara Christian
From "The Race for Theory," *Cultural Critique* 6 (Spring 1987). Reprinted with permission.

Eldridge Cleaver
From *Soul on Ice*, by Eldridge Cleaver, copyright © 1968, 1991 by Eldridge Cleaver, published by Dell Books. Reprinted by permission of the Estate of Eldridge Cleaver.

W. E. B. DuBois
From "Criteria of Negro Art," *W. E. B. DuBois: Writings*, Library of America, 1987.

bell hooks
From "The Oppositional Gaze," "Madonna," and "Representations of Whiteness in the Black Imagination," *Black Looks: Race and Representation*, South End Press, 1992.

Toni Morrison
Reprinted by permission of the publisher from *Playing in the Dark: Whiteness and the Literary Imagination* by Toni Morrison, p. 20, Cambridge, Mass.: Harvard University Press, copyright © 1992 by Toni Morrison.

Howard Thurman
From *Luminous Darkness*, Friends United Press, 1999. Reprinted with permission.

Alice Walker
From *Sent by Earth*, Seven Stories Press, 2001.

Malcolm X
From "The Ballot or the Bullet," *Malcolm X Speaks*, second edition, copyright © 1965, 1989 by Betty Shabazz and Pathfinder Press. Reprinted with permission.

CONTENTS

A NOTE ON CAPITALIZATION

Conventions governing the capitalization of racial identifiers are currently in flux. Some prefer a uniform approach of capitalizing terms referring to racial groups, such as African American, Black, Latino, or Asian American. Pseudoscientific classifications like Caucasian and Anglo-American are typically included in this practice, but more commonly used terms like "white" or "white American" are still generally not capitalized. Others adopt an all-or-nothing approach.

Although I recognize that "race" is socially constructed, for this book I have opted to capitalize racial identifiers only when I am seeking to call attention to the highly constructed, highly performative nature of "race." Using this guideline, I have not capitalized racial identifiers when they are used as adjectives or simply to refer to a group of people typically identified by that term, as in the "literature of white estrangement," "black American," or "white." My use of capitalization when I discuss White violence, Whiteness, or Blackness, on the other hand, is meant to emphasize the choice that groups of people are making about how to understand and actualize (perform) their racial identities.

ACKNOWLEDGMENTS

This book is truly a collaborative product. The seeds for it were planted in a graduate class I took at Rice University in the 1990s, when Dr. Susan Lurie included in her syllabus a little-discussed, little-regarded novel by Zora Neale Hurston, *Seraph on the Suwanee*. I never forgot that novel, or the rich conversations my peers and I had about it that semester. When I had the opportunity, I, too, taught *Seraph*. I also owe thanks to a friend who suggested, after a long semester, that I relax with *The Foxes of Harrow* by Frank Yerby, a writer whom I was unfamiliar with at the time. That recommendation introduced me to the second white life novel I had ever read, and planted a quiet question in my mind: how many of them are there? Only after encountering, quite by chance, Robert Fikes Jr.'s article "The Persistent Allure of Universality: African-American Authors of White Life Novels, 1845–1945" did I finally have a handle on what I was starting to become interested in and a place to start my reading. But none of it crystallized into a research question until I found myself rereading Martin Luther King Jr.'s "Letter from Birmingham Jail" as I prepared a fairly traditional African American literature class almost a year later. Always awed by the skill and beauty of the letter, this time, for the first time, I really *noticed* the section of the letter where King explains his deep disappointment in the White moderate. For the first time I began to understand that letter as a profound engagement with the Whiteness that structured King's world.

Since then, hundreds of books and articles about whiteness have been published. I am grateful for them all because each of them has stretched me, pushed me, and challenged me to look again at the literature I love and to recognize the long history of engagement that African American intellectuals have with Whiteness. I am particularly indebted to the work of James Baldwin, Toni Morrison, Nell Irvin Painter, David Roediger, Valerie Babb, and Grace Elizabeth Hale.

I have been fortunate to attend many conferences in the years of developing this project that have helped me bring it to fruition. I acknowledge the organizers, presenters, and attendees of the African American Literature and Culture Society Symposium; the Critical Whiteness Symposium, organized by Aimee Carillo-Rowe and the POROI staff at the

University of Iowa; the Schomburg Center for Research in Black Culture and IRADAC Conference; the Global Whiteness Conference organized by Inter-Disciplinary.net and held in Oxford, England; and the Black Women's Intellectual and Cultural History Collective Conference entitled Toward an Intellectual History of Black Women. The conversations I had and professional relationships I developed at each of these meetings have been invaluable.

There are others, however, whom I must thank by name. Laura Delbrugge helped me to recognize a book project in what seemed to my untrained eye to be random interests, and provided mentorship that helped me understand the path to becoming a published writer. Susan Boser never failed to be a partner in my thinking and writing, and I owe many of my "ah-ha" moments during this process to the long conversations we had over lunch and on the telephone.

Helen Sitler, Melissa Lingle-Martin, Crystal Machado, Gail Berlin, and Michelle Bruno—my writing group extraordinaire—provided a sounding board and critical feedback whenever I needed it. Michael T. Williamson, a generous colleague and really smart guy, helped me think through the concepts I wanted to explore in the "Occupied Territory" chapter, and although our professional relationship is young, Jolene Hubbs responded immediately when I asked her to read early drafts of that chapter. Becky Thompson has been a true champion and source of encouragement for this project since I met her at the Critical Whiteness Symposium, helping me to trust what I was seeing in the literature. And Michael Sell and James C. Trotman continue to provide inspiration for me as a scholar. Both generously reviewed chapters and offered suggestions that helped me to see my work in new ways. I will forever be grateful for the interest that each of these people took in my work, as well as the many, many others who, although unnamed, will never be forgotten.

I am grateful for the sustained support of the University Senate Research Committee, Dean Yaw Asamoah, and the School of Graduate Studies and Research at Indiana University of Pennsylvania, which has culminated in this book. I must also thank the staff at the University Press of Mississippi for their commitment to this project. This book is in the world today in no small part because of their patient and committed partnership from beginning to end.

And finally, to my family—Herbert Sr., Herbert Jr., and Zora—thank you so very much for believing I could do this, for giving me time to do this, and for loving me through this. You are my heroes.

THE SOULS OF WHITE FOLK

NAMING

The Literature of White Estrangement

We who are dark can see America in a
way that white Americans can not.
—W. E. B. Du Bois, "Criteria for Negro Art"

All attempts to repress our/black peoples' right to gaze had
produced in us an overwhelming longing to look, a rebellious desire,
an oppositional gaze. By courageously looking, we defiantly declared:
"Not only will I stare. I want my look to change reality."
—bell hooks, "The Oppositional Gaze"

In 1860, William J. Wilson, writing under the pseudonym Ethiop, published an article entitled "What Shall We Do with the White People?," an irreverent essay that turns the nineteenth-century debate about the fitness of black people for citizenship on its head by raising questions about the ability of *white* people to engage in self-government and the body politic. Ethiop argues that White Americans are marked by their persistent "discontent and disaffection," disrespect for all manifestations of humanity, and violence (58). After tracing their turbulent history, he wonders what has caused "this discontent, this unquiet state, this distress," and concludes that "Like a man who commences the life of a pick-pocket and changes not his way, becomes not only an adept in the profession, but a hardened offender . . . so also this people" (63–64). Roughly one hundred years later in 1963, Malcolm X makes a similar charge against Whiteness when he asserts that the "white world" is a "wicked world" that "thrives on indecency and immorality" ("God's Judgment," 124). He claims repeatedly that the way to "save" the white world is through the cultivation of a spirit of repentance and atonement: Whiteness must cease its evil exploitation of people of color, and it must make material amends for its wrongdoing. James Baldwin also stressed the importance of Whiteness seeking redemption for the history and legacy of racism in the world, but did so by excavating the "cost" of racism for White people. He asserts that "The guilt [of Whiteness] remains, more deeply rooted, more securely lodged, than the oldest of old fears," and that this weight has caused a near fatal "distance from his conscience—from himself" within the White American ("Guilt," 409–410).

Between 1860 and 1965, writers as diverse as Paul Laurence Dunbar, Zora Neale Hurston, Richard Wright, and Ann Petry—who have all been identified as exhibiting a Black nationalist consciousness at points in their careers—each published novels that focused on white lives. In 1995 Robert Fikes Jr., a librarian at San Diego State University, identified enough of these "unusual" texts that he coined the term "white life novel" to capture the "persistence" of Black authors writing fictional texts that revolved primarily around White characters (105). In addition to the canonical authors mentioned above, Fikes's first article on the subject, "Escaping the Literary Ghetto: African American Authors of White Life Novels, 1946–1994," mentions more than twenty titles that fall into this category, including pieces by little-known, little-read authors like William T. Attaway, Adam Clayton Powell Sr., Chancellor J. Williams, and William Gardner Smith. The identification of the long history and wide range of "white life" work took another significant leap forward with David Roediger's 1998 compilation, *Black on White: Black Writers on What It Means to Be White*, which included fifty-one selections from a number of different genres and media, including photography and graphic art. Roediger even includes excerpts that focus on white characters from longer pieces that are not necessarily white life works, like the section from Frederick Douglass's 1845 *Narrative* on the mistress of the plantation, Mrs. Auld. Easily, then, we can identify African American writings about Whiteness that date at least as far back as the 1840s—over 170 years of production. These writings include more than twenty specifically white life novels identified by Fikes and more than forty white life texts represented in Roediger's collection. Over thirty authors are represented in just these two publications, and yet African American thinking and writings about Whiteness have never been thought of as making up a tradition within African American letters.

Not all literature about white lives is equally illuminating. Some pieces, although they may feature white characters, do not offer a critical view of Whiteness or seek to explore the meaning of that racial identity for those who so identify. Those are not the texts with which I concern myself in this book. I am seeking here to identify and name a very particular tradition within African American literature in which authors explore Whiteness as a racialized subjectivity.

Among these texts, Whiteness emerges as a way of seeing and knowing the world that masquerades as universality and remains largely unnamed and unrecognized. It is exposed as a mode of social organization that is shaped by skin-color privilege and that is inextricably enmeshed with other vectors of identity such as gender, class, sexual orientation, and the organization of space. At a very basic level, the texts I'm interested in represent Whiteness as a positionality, or perspective, that refuses to acknowledge its own narrowness, its alarmingly consistent history of oppression, its contradictions and failures. Like contemporary scholars Owen J. Dwyer and John Paul Jones III, this genre of literature helps us to recognize Whiteness as "an *epistemology* . . . a particular way of knowing and valuing social life" that "relies upon an essentialist and non-relational understanding of identity" (210). These insights into, analyses of, and arguments about Whiteness are consistent across the range of texts I term the "literature of white estrangement."[1]

The literature of white estrangement (or the literature of white exposure; I use the terms interchangeably) is the larger collection of materials from practically every conceivable written genre—including short fiction, sermons, journalism, essays, drama, critical texts, and poetry—that critically engages Whiteness as a social construction. Each of the texts that make up the tradition, with their own particular critical, historical, and sociological nuances, makes visible the unseen, unspoken, and unevaluated nature of Whiteness. They challenge the myths and mythologies of Whiteness and the meanings that are ascribed to it within American society at various historical moments by forcing readers to confront the regressive, destructive, and often uncivilized "nature" of Whiteness as it is constructed in their worlds. Many texts within the tradition are also implicitly aimed toward white readers, part of an effort to engage white people in the process of reflecting upon their own lives and culture. This authorial intent is captured most directly by the words of Charles Chesnutt, who stated, "If I do write, I shall write for a purpose. . . . The object of my writings would be not so much the elevation of the colored people as the elevation of the whites," and is implied in a comment like the one made by Hurston in a letter to author and photographer Carl Van Vechten, "I have hopes of breaking that silly rule about Negroes not writing about white people" (Chesnutt, *Journals*, 139; Hurston, *Life in Letters*, 467). The recently recovered journals of Texas writer Lillian B. Horace offer a similar insight into the goals of an African American author focusing on Whiteness: "to give a true picture of life not only Negro but with regard to white life . . ."; and novelist Frank Yerby commented on the subversive messaging of his fiction when he said in an interview, "Look, if your only theme is 'Oh, God, I'm Black and look how badly they treat me,' people get tired of that. You have to be a little more subtle than that," suggesting the quantity and quality of thought he had devoted to the question of how to reach his largely white reading audience (Horace, *Diary*, 112; Maryemma Graham, 70). What these statements suggest is that this genre of writing has often been envisioned and utilized by African American intellectuals as a deliberate strategy for reaching white readers who perhaps would not otherwise have engaged their critiques of racism, social inequality, and injustice. The literature of white estrangement attempts the important critical project of unveiling Whiteness *to itself* by providing a revealing counternarrative to the myths of Whiteness.

Much of the literature of white estrangement has not been engaged by contemporary scholars or celebrants of African American literature. Indeed, before the 1990s this body of literature was not generally read, anthologized, taught, or theorized.[2] The reasons for this unfortunate fact are myriad, but three explanations are especially significant. First are the ways that African American literature is defined, limited, and marketed, which has been commented upon by writer-critics Langston Hughes, Zora Neale Hurston,[3] Robert Fikes Jr., and more recently Ward Connerly, chairman of the politically conservative American Civil Rights Institute. Connerly argued in a 2000 op-ed piece, "Where 'Separate But Equal' Still Rules," that "one of the last bastions of segregation in America today" is "your local bookstore." Outraged that his book "recount[ing] the story of . . . [his] advocacy against racial preferences" had been shelved in the African American interest section, he charges that the practice of marketing and shelving titles according to the author's "race" is financially damaging to writers and potentially misleading to consumers. He goes on to assert:

> But the economic harm pales in contrast to the intellectual and cultural damage caused by the bookstores' version of racial profiling. They have fallen into the trap of thinking that a writer's skin color is a reliable guide to judging the contents of his or her books. . . . By relying on a blatant stereotype—that blacks are the only ones interested in the history, culture and

politics of black people—the bookstores marginalize some writers and limit
their ability to reach out to a broader audience and to share common bonds
and values. (23)

Connerly suggests here that the marketing of Black-authored texts has
become prescriptive rather than descriptive, built on social expectations of
African American interests and knowledge bases. The author's skin color
or "culture," if it is something other than unmarked "Whiteness," defines
the placement of certain texts, which not only shapes readers' expectations of what constitutes "Black literature" but also affects their ability to
engage or avoid it. Our understanding of literature is deeply influenced by
these narrowly proscribed geographical and ideological templates developed and deployed within the literary marketplace. This "version of racial
profiling," as Connerly terms it, racializes an intellectual space that one
would perhaps prefer to be colorblind; the establishment of discrete areas
that respond to the presumed interests of people of color creates, in effect,
a limited-access highway that cordons off the varied intellectual contributions of writers of color.

Second and closely related to the first are issues of audience reception.
The hegemonic reading public has had difficulty understanding "what to
do with" the literature of white estrangement. Echoing Connerly's analysis, Fikes argues in "How Major Book Review Editors Stereotype Black
Authors" that part of the reason black and white readers seem confounded
by white life novels is that the promotional patterns of the mainstream
press "reinforce the majority group perception that blacks are experts on
themselves and little else" (110). David Roediger concurs, noting, "Writers
of color, and most notably African-American writers, are cast as providing insight, often presumed to be highly subjective, of what it is like to
be 'a minority'" (4). Joseph McElrath and Robert Leitz III take a different
approach in understanding the reception of texts from this tradition. In
their study of the rise and fall of Chesnutt's literary influence, they conclude that white readers reached a point where they "were not interested
in paying to be scolded" (23). Both of these explanations are central to
understanding why the literature of white estrangement generally failed to
enter the cultural conversations of their day, and why the books fell out of
print so quickly after publication. The white reading and literary communities of the nineteenth through mid-twentieth centuries were generally
unprepared by their society to accept African American authors as lively
intellectuals with broad literary interests and capacities. Consequently,

they were more likely to expect black writers to have a limited range of materials that they could effectively engage. Given their inability and unwillingness to recognize the broad range of black expertise, White readers saw the literature of white exposure as a source of anxiety, as their expectations of Black knowledge and achievement were challenged. Their discomfort at having their beliefs about Blackness unsettled was then further compounded by the fact that the literary texts of this tradition offered less than flattering images of Whiteness, making it more likely that those messages would be ignored and would lose the financial support of the reading public. White readers did not long invest in black literature that challenged the images they had constructed of Blackness or the mythologies they had created of Whiteness.

African American readers, on the other hand, were not drawn to texts that featured White protagonists and storylines for different reasons. Seeking content that both validated and illuminated our experiences and existence in the United States, historically fiction from the literature of white estrangement simply did not satisfy our reasons for reading. Socially and politically, African Americans *needed* voices and representations that challenged the often racist misrepresentations of Blackness that were being disseminated during most of the eighteenth and nineteenth centuries, and a good portion of the twentieth. We needed writing that gave us back pieces of ourselves and that laid the groundwork for social revolution and change, and we needed Black people who could speak in the public arena, where so many had previously been silenced. White life literature was too easily perceived as abandoning the struggle for civil rights in favor of personal gain, a version of literary "passing" that allowed the individual to achieve social acceptance by disavowing his or her connection to the African American community. Thus, some of the harshest critics of white life fiction have been the black press, critics, and reviewers, who often offered backhanded praise, at best, for these texts.

The final piece to the puzzle of why the literature of white estrangement has not been engaged more fully is the reception that these texts have traditionally received from scholarly communities engaged in African American and American literature and culture. Because these texts resist traditional categorization as well as standard disciplinary and theoretical approaches, professionals in these fields, like their lay counterparts, do not quite know how to engage them, making it easier to overlook them as a genre of writing. Highlighting the "almost utter failure to encourage or even notice studies of whiteness by scholars of color," Roediger writes that the "serious 'white life novel' has left very little impact on American literary criticism" (8). The early work of Henry Louis Gates Jr. also reminds us that the racially charged context of the United States had significant effects on the ways that African American writing was conceived as well as received; this politicized context initially helped to define what was accepted, and later, what was acceptable.[4] The literature of white estrangement did not conform to these definitions and was all but "disappeared"[5] by essentialist paradigms that narrowly conceptualized African American literature as "black writers writing about Black subjects," or "black writers representing the Black Experience." The paradigms by which most of us were trained until quite recently, and the realities and practices that have shaped the African American canon, have led scholars to aggressively dismiss African American writing that does not conform to this formula. In the words of Claudia Tate, novels deemed "not black enough" were cast aside by scholars of both American and African American literature and culture (4).

The structures of exclusion at work in African American canon formation are nowhere more apparent than in the work of Zora Neale Hurston, a gifted and prolific artist and intellectual who was both an architect and a product of the Harlem Renaissance. An artist with a tremendous and controversial vision and an insatiable interest in the wide range of humanity and human expression, she ran afoul of many of the agenda makers of the Harlem Renaissance largely because her work did not present or "protest" the racial injustices African Americans were facing in the 1920s and 1930s. She was openly critical of black leadership that continually cast African Americans as victims of racial circumstance and believed so completely in the value of Black culture that she focused almost exclusively on its beauty, integrity, and self-sufficiency. For her stubborn refusal to represent the dispossessed black subject, her work was often rejected by her contemporaries. Richard Wright famously dismissed the now canonical *Their Eyes Were Watching God* as superfluous fiction and charged that *Eyes* was "not addressed to the Negro, but to a white audience whose chauvinistic tastes she knows how to satisfy" ("Between Laughter," 25). Alain Locke, who was a mentor and friend of Hurston, lamented that she had not "come to grips with motive fiction and social document fiction" (18). In both cases, Hurston was taken to task because her representation of Black life did not easily serve the movement's political goals. Although other reviews of *Eyes* were more favorable, Hurston was effectively blacklisted by these two giants of African American literature and *criticism*. She was victimized by the strict policing of the African American canon in the 1930s, and this was even before she published her final novel, a white life fiction entitled *Seraph on the Suwanee*. By the time she published *Seraph*, Hurston had already been firmly ejected from the African American literary and social communities that had supported her earlier in her career.

Much of the scholarship that dismisses or ignores African American writing on Whiteness follows a line of reasoning articulated in the mid-1940s by reviewer Philip Butcher, who characterized several white life works as "raceless" because they did not focus on African American lives. Building on that foundation, in 1958 Robert Bone labeled any African American author who did not seek to "achieve universality through a sensitive interpretation of his own culture" "assimilationist," essentially claiming that any text that failed to exhibit sufficient traces of "Negro nationalism" grew out of "an unconscious desire to be white, coupled with feelings of revulsion toward the Negro masses" (2). In an article entitled "The Persistent Allure of Universality," Fikes describes this literature as "consciously race neutral," while Claudia Tate labels the white life novels in her study "anomalies, primarily because they resist, to varying degrees, the race and gender paradigms that we . . . impose on black textuality" (Fikes, 226; Tate, 8). Shelley Fisher Fishkin refers to that same group of texts (as well as those white-authored books that feature black characters and/or African American life) as "transgressive" (130). More recently, Gene Andrew Jarrett, editor of *African American Literature Beyond Race: An Alternative Reader*, author of *Deans and Truants: Race and Realism in African American Literature*, and one of very few scholars to engage these literary texts in a book-length work, acknowledged his preference for the term "anomaly" for the reasons articulated by Tate. While these taxonomic efforts have provided a starting point for understanding the aggressive dismissal these text have experienced, they all seem to downplay or miss altogether two crucial points: (1) that the tradition of black writing that dissects and analyzes Whiteness extends beyond the field of literature and, therefore, may be doing something more than simply enacting a resistance to the prevailing definitions of "race literature" or "Black literature"; and (2) that writing about Whiteness might be a strategic engagement with the discourse(s) of White supremacy prevalent at a particular historical moment.

The Souls of White Folk attempts, for the first time, to conceptualize a broad range of African American engagements with Whiteness—the private musings and the publicly shared work—as an intellectual tradition that has proceeded within African American literature and letters for more than a century and a half. It is an effort to call attention to the literature of white exposure as an identifiable and sustained tradition of interrogation and resistance, to name the "long-standing liberatory efforts of African Americans from the past (and present) who fought (and fight) the good fight against white hegemony and injustice" (Yancy, 18). But perhaps "tradition" is the wrong language to invoke here. My sense is that these authors were not so much reading and "talking to" each other about Whiteness as responding to the specific justifications and rationales of Whiteness being offered at a particular moment in time. The fact that their analyses have an uncanny consistency, or that their arguments resonate over time, says more about the ways that Whiteness has historically been constructed in the United States[6] than it does about their knowledge of each other's work or their conscious attempts to build upon the work of the African American artists and intellectuals who preceded them. Indeed, I have found little evidence in the letters, diaries, autobiographies, and critical materials that I have consulted that many of these writers knew much about other authors who contributed to this tradition or the content of the other productions. They themselves did not seem to know of the long history of African American intellectual engagement with Whiteness. Our efforts as scholars and critics, however, can bring to light the groundbreaking work that African Americans have done in helping us to understand Whiteness more deeply and fully than perhaps we thought possible.

The literature of white estrangement is deployed in a few different ways in this book. First, I rely largely on the nonfictional work—essays, sermons, scholarly publications, journal entries, and the like—within this tradition to provide a theoretical base for my explorations of texts that Fikes identified as "white life novels." This approach is perhaps most clearly in use in chapter 1, where I reclaim Du Bois's interest in white psychology and the medical discourses of his day as a way of reading a turn-of-the-century, social reform novel penned by another writer. Similarly, in chapter 3 I use writings from this tradition to provide a framework in which to understand the connections between race, space, (white) identity, and violence suggested by a Civil Rights–era memoir. In both cases, the literature of white estrangement becomes the theoretical framework that enables a deeper engagement with the analyses of White psychology and sociology offered by the literary texts. Second, drawing from Barbara Christian's assertion that "people of color have always theorized—but in forms quite different from the Western form of abstract logic . . . our theorizing . . . is often in narrative forms, in the stories we create," I examine white life novels themselves as theory, narratives that provide a metadiscourse for understanding or explaining some aspect of Whiteness (68). This strategy is at use primarily in chapter 2, where I consider the insights into white womanhood and White femininity that are offered by two white life novels published in the 1940s, texts that extend our knowledge of the intersections of race (here coded as Whiteness), gender, and class. The third and final approach to the literature of white estrangement that I employ in this book is to bring current theoretical approaches to bear on it, primarily from the broad field of critical whiteness studies. This approach is found primarily in chapter 3, where I consider if the literature of white estrangement has already taken us beyond our current understandings of the connection between space and race that are being articulated within cultural and social geography. My goal here is to demonstrate the contemporary relevance of the literature of white estrangement and to highlight not only its prescience, but also the continuing ways it extends the frontiers of what we think we know and understand about Whiteness.

I have made the rather unorthodox decision to use different approaches to the literature of white exposure in each chapter to suggest the breadth of possibility in utilizing these texts, and the wealth of knowledge that has remained largely unrecognized and untapped. In all of these approaches, however, I am seeking to activate a dialogue that has been a century and a half in the making, the bridging of two critical areas of exploration and inquiry, African American (literary) studies and critical whiteness studies. In so doing, I hope to reveal the grounds upon which African American intellectuals have challenged the myths, lies, and distortions of Whiteness in an attempt to rewrite the present and future of race relations in America.

I also remain consistently interested in how the literature of white estrangement intervenes in particular articulations of Whiteness at given historical moments. While the literature of white exposure as well as contemporary scholars have pointed out the consistency of the exploitative and oppressive practices of Whiteness (an issue that I take up explicitly in the conclusion of this book), the sheer volume of historical and sociological analyses of Whiteness demonstrate the ways that Whiteness adapts, changes, and rearticulates itself to retain its social ascendency and to minimize the challenges to its supremacy that constantly surface. Because Whiteness is not a static, unchanging, racialized subjectivity, this book is also, at least in part, a period study covering three distinct themes. Chapter 1 focuses on 1880–1910 and the work of W. E. B. Du Bois and Charles Chesnutt. Both writers explore the concept of "double consciousness," a term that was still evolving, being debated and revised, at the time that Du Bois fixed its meaning in scholarly and popular lexicons. Examining the discourses of neurasthenia that were popular at the time, I consider how these authors countered cultural scripts of White superiority and refinement with images of a Whiteness that was emotionally and psychologically frail, schizophrenic in its sociopolitical goals for the nation, and often brutish and self-delusional. In so doing they challenged assumptions about the fitness for leadership of elite Whites and sought to bring the realities of racial inequity and oppression to bear on the conceptualization of America's future.

In chapter 2 I turn my attention to the 1930s and 1940s, a period of tremendous instability and uncertainty in America. These decades witnessed a world war, an economic meltdown so catastrophic that it was dubbed the Great Depression, increased agitation for social change from various ethnic minority groups and labor organizations, and a complete transformation in social norms and expectations for women. It is the latter point with which this chapter largely concerns itself. Examining two white life novels published in this period, Frank Yerby's *The Foxes of Harrow* and Zora Neale Hurston's *Seraph on the Suwanee*, I consider their engagement with the cultural debate about the appropriate role of White women in American society. At a time when women were being told through a range of media that their "proper place" was again in the home (after a period of being encouraged to enter the workforce as part of their patriotic duty), both Yerby and Hurston create narratives that subversively explore the psychological and emotional costs that women pay to conform to this ideal of White femininity. Not only were they politicizing the white home and family at a time when mainstream culture was dissembling their efforts at the same, but they were also theorizing White women's positions in and responsibility for the racial and social hierarchies of the United States.

Chapter 3 brings my engagement with the literature of white exposure to the turbulent period of the 1960s, where I examine the issues of white violence, space, and race. Scholars and activists working in these areas have posited a powerful connection between race and space, highlighting that the control of space allows Whiteness to create "race" in very particular ways. The memoir of the Little Rock Nine's Melba Beals, *Warriors Don't Cry*, and the writings of Civil Rights activists Terrence Roberts, Carlotta

Walls Lanier, Howard Thurman, and John Lewis, however, challenge us to recognize that Whiteness is not simply using space to create race in ways that are advantageous to itself, but that its organization of space is an inextricable part of how Whiteness understands itself. These texts suggest that space, place, and violence are constitutive elements of the identity of Whiteness, and I argue that we need a new conceptual framework that recognizes the racialization of space as a primary mechanism by which Whiteness comes to know itself as distinctively human.

Although these writers—this tradition—were perhaps some of the first intellectuals to theorize Whiteness, their work in these areas is little recognized, little known. Nevertheless, their conversations have been carried over decades, even centuries, and have built on each other over time. This consistent attentiveness to the discourses of Whiteness has meant that when the expectations and standards for acceptable social behavior have shifted—sometimes through very public, direct, or violent means—African American intellectuals have been there to witness and chronicle the subsequent crises of Whiteness and to record the fevered attempts to shore up, reinstate, and reinforce racial structures that seem on the verge of collapse. Positioned as they have been on the outside of America's cultural mythologies and national discourses, both as participants and creators, they have been astute observer-critics of the shifting epistemologies, ideologies, and rationale of Whiteness. Marginalized but not excluded, perhaps the most common, and certainly the most accepted responses they have produced have been narratives that focus on African American responses to racial and social inequality and injustice. However, this is only part of the history of African American literary production in the United States. The literature of white estrangement was another concrete way to critique and challenge the exploitative politics of race in the United States. *The Souls of White Folk* is another piece of the story.

Chapter One

"A FORM OF INSANITY WHICH OVERTAKES WHITE MEN"

W. E. B. Du Bois, Charles Chesnutt, and the Specter of White Double Consciousness

What is most terrible is that American white men are not prepared to
believe my version of the story, to believe that it happened. In order to
avoid believing that, they have to set up in themselves a fantastic system
of evasions, denials, and justifications, which system is about to destroy
their grasp of reality, which is another way of saying their moral sense.
—James Baldwin, "The White Problem"

The issue at stake is to find a way by which fear is abandoned and men
are free to act responsibly as citizens in the first instance and as citizens
committed to values that are moral and ethical in the second instance.
—Howard Thurman, *The Luminous Darkness*

In 1903, W. E. B. Du Bois published the now classic *The Souls of Black Folk*. In the Forethought, he explains that he wrote the book to explore the "problem of the Twentieth Century . . . the color-line" by "outlin[ing] the two worlds within and without the Veil" (359). In these profound words that begin his treatise, Du Bois signals his primary concern with race—which he understood more as a sociocultural or sociohistorical divide than a biologically based difference between people—in the United States. It was a conversation both timely and daring at the turn of the twentieth century, for in the early 1900s the country was still struggling to understand and constitute its post–Civil War identity. Citizens black and white were struggling to come to terms with the meaning of the sociopolitical revolution that had ended slavery and, however briefly, enabled African American political power, while leaving the mantra of White supremacy intact.

The Souls of Black Folk is a meditation on the social and psychological impact of racial inequality on African Americans. Du Bois writes,

> After the Egyptian and Indian, the Greek and Roman, the Teuton and Mongolian, the Negro is a sort of seventh son, born with a veil, and gifted with second-sight in this American world,—a world which yields him no true self-consciousness, but only lets him see himself through the revelation of the other world. It is a peculiar sensation, this double-consciousness, this sense of always looking at one's self through the eyes of others, of measuring one's soul by the tape of a world that looks on in amused contempt and pity. One ever feels his two-ness,—an American, a Negro; two warring souls, two thoughts, two unreconciled strivings; two warring ideals in one dark body, whose dogged strength alone keeps it from being torn asunder. (364–365)

Double consciousness is one result, perhaps the most pernicious effect, of the color line. It is the two-ness that is born when one's self-understanding collides with social constructions of race that limit one's ability to actualize one's vision of the self. Double consciousness leads to the wasting of talents and energies: talents that are underutilized or ignored because of the social designation and/or skin color of people of African descent; energies that are expended in anger, frustration, or despair or in attempts to excel in a system designed to prevent the advancement of a particular group based solely on racial classification. The racial caste system of the United States has "wrought sad havoc with the courage and faith and deeds" of African Americans (366). Du Bois argues that, for Black Americans, the lack of full acceptance and valuing of all aspects of their identity is the catalyst for a psychic rupture that is a source of enduring and often debilitating pain.

Yet, when Du Bois relates the anecdote of exchanging visiting cards with girls at his school as a child, he also acknowledges the possibility for double consciousness to be a source of protection for the black subject. As "one girl, a tall newcomer" refuses his card "peremptorily, with a glance," the young Du Bois understands himself as different, understands that he is not accepted, not *recognized* by the White world (364). He sees "the veil" that separates White and Black America and knows that he is not considered a human equal by many on the other side of the divide. It is a realization that initially fills him with the desire to out-achieve his white peers rather than tear down the veil. For a precious short while he holds the White world "in common contempt," living "above it in a region of blue sky" (364). Although he has been initiated into an awareness of a racialized world, double consciousness protects his fragile ego and allows him to be secure in his own humanity and to believe in his own worth. Soon enough, however, his desire for all that Whiteness offers overshadows his disdain, and he is left with full knowledge of his marginalization and the limitations many would place upon him due to his socially ascribed race.

But what of the little White girl who refused his visiting card? How had the color line shaped her psyche? If double consciousness is a psychologically and emotionally traumatic result of the racial divide, what effects does the color line have on White group psychology? While central to the literature of white estrangement, these questions have only been marginally engaged by contemporary scholars of critical whiteness studies. Instead, scholarship from this field has produced important analyses of the ways in which Whiteness has been reproduced, naturalized, and deployed during various historical moments. The field has also illuminated how efforts to rationalize and maintain White sociopolitical supremacy have intersected with a variety of other rhetorical and disciplinary efforts to legitimate racial difference and hierarchy, such as those coming from science, religion, philosophy, and economics.[1] However, Du Bois's groundbreaking work on the effects of racism on Black Americans urges me to engage Whiteness from a different angle. I want to ask not only "How have White people benefited from the racial politics of this country?" I also want to understand what psychological, spiritual, and emotional effects the color line has produced in White Americans.[2]

The concept of double consciousness is, of course, not original to Du Bois. In his book *W. E. B. Du Bois and American Political Thought*, Adolph L. Reed usefully outlines the range of intellectuals and artists who utilized the term prior to and during Du Bois's lifetime.[3] But unlike Henry B. Wonham, author of "Howells, Du Bois, and the Effect of 'Common-Sense': Race, Realism, and Nervousness in *An Imperative Duty* and *The Souls of Black Folk*," who stresses the "rich cultural exchange [that happened] between writers on opposite sides of the color line," Reed concludes that "attempts to establish direct links . . . would require very elaborate arguments and layers of supposition and presumption. Nor would they—even if arguably successful in establishing some plausible, though remote tie—shed much light either on Du Bois's thinking or his relation to his contemporary world" (Wonham, 129; Reed, 105). Tracing lines of direct influence might, indeed, prove nearly impossible, but there is no doubt that a fuller appreciation of Du Bois's reworking of double consciousness is possible when one considers the full range of contexts in which it was being used at the turn of the twentieth century. The disciplines of philosophy, history, psychology, and various fields of medicine were all exploring the concept of a "divided self," if not specifically appropriating the term. Indeed, as Dickson Bruce points out in "W. E. B. Du Bois and the Idea of Double Consciousness," the concept had been "the subject of rather extensive experimentation and debate for at least seventy-five years" by the time Du Bois reframed it, and the great public intellectual was undoubtedly attracted to the discourse because of how richly dynamic, malleable, and contested the term was (303). It is also likely, however, that Du Bois was drawn to this particular cultural conversation because of the ways in which the discourse of double consciousness was being racialized, particularly by the white medical community of his time, to exclude people of color. Writings about double consciousness provide ample evidence that modernity was being framed and debated by white intellectuals and cultural elites as if considerations of racial and social justice were inconsequential; their work evidences a willed ignorance of the significant role that race would play in either accelerating or arresting American progress. The fact that the meaning of "double consciousness" was not yet fixed, and that there was still space in which to intervene, shape, and reconceptualize it, meant that it could be made to serve a different agenda. Thus, Du Bois's rearticulation of double consciousness in terms of the experiences of African-descended people was one way of challenging the narrow and regressive conceptualizations of race of his time. This haunting connection between Du Bois's work and the medical, psychological, and philosophical theories of white Americans of the late nineteenth and early twentieth centuries suggests that there is much to be gained from reconsidering Du Bois's interest in White double consciousness.[4]

Writing around the same time but at the end of his career, author Charles Chesnutt was also thinking about double consciousness. Two years after the publication of *The Souls of Black Folk*, Chesnutt's final novel, *The Colonel's Dream*, was released to mixed reviews and poor sales. Yet, the white life novel is an extraordinary literary extension of many of the deliberations Du Bois was working out early in his career. Like Du Bois, Chesnutt was thinking about how the racial past continues to shape the present and future of the nation. He was concerned with the ways in which the atrocities and injustices of slavery in America were being whitewashed and forgotten in the name of sectional reconciliation, and he was outraged that people of color were still being discounted and largely prohibited from becoming productive, contributing citizens and intellectuals. Chesnutt also believed, as did Du Bois, that "the problem of the color line" was not strictly or even primarily located with Black Americans (Du Bois, *Souls of Black Folk*, 359). As such, Chesnutt sought to understand the sources of white anxiety around race and the emotions and habits of mind that explained racial animosity, white violence, and white indifference to the suffering of people of color. With a solid belief that through his writing he could "head a determined, organized crusade against" the "unjust" racial caste system of the United States, at the end of his writing career he joined the public discourse surrounding White double consciousness (*Journals*, 140).

Du Bois and Chesnutt problematized the concept of double consciousness on at least two levels. First, they both entered the cultural conversation about the "divided self" by engaging intellectuals of their time on their own terms, that is, by thinking about the sources and implications of *White* double consciousness. To appreciate their interventions at this level necessitates that we engage the explanations of neurasthenia that were being advanced by the white medical community in the early twentieth century. Here we can discern, as Du Bois and Chesnutt did before us, an ephemeral but traceable anxiety that hints at the dis-ease of Whiteness in an already pluralist nation. The second approach they deployed to transform the discourse around White double consciousness was to challenge the assertion that white social, cultural, and political elites were better suited than others to lead the United States into the next period of sociopolitical development. Du Bois and Chesnutt framed White double consciousness as a malaise—one that threatened not only the individual but also national progress and development. In both cases the authors exposed the racialized assumptions and ideologies at work in the discourse of White double consciousness and demonstrated the folly of concentrating power in the hands of a group who, by virtue of a medical discourse that they had advanced, had already acknowledged their inability to adapt to the challenges of modern life.

By the late 1800s a new diagnosis, nervous diathesis, dominated medical discourse in the United States. Affecting many of the most recognized artists and intellectuals of the time, neurasthenia, as it was more commonly known, was a supple and malleable disorder that encompassed a wide range of symptoms under its conceptual umbrella—from insomnia and irritability to chronic headaches and epilepsy, sometimes culminating in paralysis and insanity. Men and women, young and old, were equally susceptible; those who were well established and those still striving to become members of the cultural elite. Neurasthenia seemed to affect almost everyone who was awake and paying attention to the rapid cultural shifts happening in American society at the end of the nineteenth century. By the time of Du Bois's publication of *The Souls of Black Folk* in 1903, the condition had become a cultural marker of distinction and refinement. For people of the late nineteenth and early twentieth centuries, being diagnosed as a neurasthenic meant that one was a sensitive and reflective person, albeit one who was (understandably) having difficulty navigating the changing norms and expectations of modern American life.

Dr. George Miller Beard perhaps did more to advance neurasthenia as a medical diagnosis and a cultural term than anyone else. A neurologist by training and practice, he began to explore neurasthenia when, "like other neurologists of his day, [he] . . . discovered that a large proportion of his patients complained not of clearly-defined ailments, but of vague and unclassifiable symptoms, of morbid anxiety, unaccountable fatigue, irrational fears, of erratic sexual behavior" (Rosenberg, 247). After further study, he classified a whole range of ailments under the term "nervous diathesis," claiming that they all were diseases of the "central or peripheral nervous system" (Beard, 25). Like medieval formulations of the humors that were believed to regulate human temperament and mental and physical health, the nervous system at the turn of the twentieth century was understood to be the seat of bodily, and thus psychological, well-being. When the system was in balance, being expended and replenished appropriately, the body and mind could maintain health. But when the system was overtaxed and unable to sustain all the demands that were placed upon it, physical and mental deterioration could result. Thus, neurasthenia asserted a connection between the body, the environment, and the psyche—a way of thinking about human psychology (and physiology) that gained significant credibility under Sigmund Freud. Unlike Freud, however, these early medical doctors believed that the stresses of a changing modern society—anything from technological advances like the advent of the telegraph and steam power to rapid shifts in social class—could trigger the disorder in certain classes of people. Once afflicted, patients could anticipate lifelong management of the disease in an effort to limit relapses and further debilitation. This was Beard's signature contribution to the field of neurology, advanced by doctors around the world until well into the 1920s. Beard published widely (if not repetitively) on the topic, including his tour de force, *American Nervousness: Its Causes and Consequences* (1881). He intended this last contribution to be the most accessible, and he wrote it for the audience of everyday Americans who wanted to know more about the disease that seemed to define their age.

Neurasthenia achieved social and medical ascendancy in part because many of the most influential social, cultural, and intellectual leaders of the early modern era—including Theodore Roosevelt, Edith Wharton, Emma Goldman, Mary Wilkins Freeman, Theodore Dreiser, and Henry Adams—all suffered from the disorder (Lutz, 15). Yet, while its debilitating effects certainly could be disruptive, neurasthenia was never stigmatized, and thus there was never any sense that the disease automatically made one unfit for leadership. In fact, Beard claimed just the opposite in *American Nervousness*, arguing that neurasthenia made one significantly *more* suited to leadership roles because it evidenced one's superior intellectual and emotional constitution. It externalized and made visible, in effect, the internal, superior lineage and "blood" of the White cultural elite. Thus, nervousness became one's claim to a right of rule, a right to sit at the tables where America's future was being envisioned.

It is all the more significant, but perhaps not surprising, then, that Beard's conceptualization of neurasthenia was heavily influenced by contemporary understandings of and biases about race, class, and gender. This was so much the case that Tom Lutz comments in his seminal study of neurasthenia, *American Nervousness, 1903*, "The class, race, and gender biases encoded in the neurasthenic [diagnosis] demonstrate that socially constructed practices and positions determined who, how, and why one becomes diseased" (20). Neurasthenia was a comfortable companion to the scientific racism that dominated nineteenth- and early-twentieth-century intellectual discourse, a time when social Darwinists were still arguing that "lesser" races should be allowed to "naturally" decline so that the fitter Caucasian race could thrive, biologists were using cranial measurements to explain the purported lagging intellectual development of "Negroes," and scholars in the nascent field of sociology were classifying humankind into superior, and, of course, inferior, races. Neurasthenia simply built upon the commonsense understandings of racial difference that had been elevated to scientific "fact" by this time. Beard did not question white American superiority in his field of neurology any more than the majority of physicians in the 1930s and 1940s doubted that the blood of white and black Americans should be segregated in blood banks.[5] In fact, the racist foundation of his conception of neurasthenia is explicit in his explanation of who is susceptible to the disease: "The fine organization is distinguished from the coarse by fine, soft hair, delicate skin, nicely chiselled features, small bones, tapering extremities, and frequently by a muscular system comparatively small and feeble" (26). As Toni Morrison has argued of the Africanist presence in American literature—that it is often a backdrop by which white characters come to know themselves—this description gains its force of persuasion by an implied contrast with an unnamed Other who is figured as antithetical to the White subject (*Playing*, 51). The "fine, soft hair, delicate skin" and "nicely chiselled features" are implicitly compared with races and ethnicities for whom this physical description would not generally apply. Later in *American Nervousness* Beard explicitly excludes the "North American barbarian" (Native Americans) and the "negro," by virtue of their "immature mind[s]" and "savagery," from those who can be affected by nervous diathesis. His reason: their presumed inferiority (130–131). As a scientist, the most he would allow is that as the "less civilized" people of the world became more educated and refined, there would likely be a concomitant increase in nervous disorders among them, too.

Thus, race is a subtext for Beard's conceptualization of American nervousness. Importantly, it also became a mechanism for diagnosing the disease. Any physician who recognized neurasthenia as a legitimate medical diagnosis also, as a matter of course, bought into the discourse of White superiority. African Americans might be afflicted with a number of physiological and psychological ailments, but they were not often diagnosed as neurasthenic.[6] Beard's understanding of nervous diathesis reflected as well as shaped the racial discourse of his time, reinforcing White supremacy as a "common-sense" approach to understanding the modern world. Culturally, the disease carved out an imaginative space within which only White Americans could exist, leading the disease to be reappropriated as a marker of social and cultural elevation. It also supported a vision of White America as uniquely conditioned for the work of reshaping American society and best suited for the work of moving America into her promising future.

Beard believed that neurasthenia was a consequence of modern advances and the freedom of a youthful and unfettered America. Charles Rosenberg argues in his introduction to the 1972 republication of Beard's *American Nervousness* that "Beard's doctrine of nervous exhaustion was . . . a nationalistic concept" that essentially celebrated the superiority of

American social, cultural, and industrial accomplishments (n.p.). However, those advances often required the rethinking of established systems of belief and ways of being in the world. Not only were new technologies emerging that brought the world into much closer intellectual and physical proximity, but expectations about work and leisure, religion and spirituality, success and failure, the roles of men and women and of black and white citizens were also, consequently, changing rapidly. On the heels of the Civil War and the ending of slavery, newly enfranchised African Americans were being educated, asserting their political voices and rights, and migrating from the South in numbers previously unknown; women, who had become much more socially and politically active in the early to mid-nineteenth century, were continuing to transform themselves through their embrace of the "New Woman" ideal; and immigration, urban population growth, and industrialization were transforming the focuses of power in the United States in previously unimagined ways. It was a time of tremendous flux, and what nervous exhaustion evidenced as much as anything was the inability of White Americans to adapt to and work through those changes. Without the veneer of White supremacist assumptions, nervousness begins look like what it actually was, a psychological infirmity that manifested among people who were having trouble negotiating the demands and realities of social change. The discourse of neurasthenia, however, rhetorically and culturally masked the inflexibility of Whiteness. Without it, the tenets of White racial superiority would have faced serious ideological challenges. People might have begun to wonder why America's future was being entrusted to the guardianship of such a distraught White elite.

At least one physician broke ranks and advanced a theory of neurasthenia that read it as social debilitation rather than distinction. Dissatisfied with the "multiform variations" that medicine had settled on in its understanding of neurasthenia and "seeking to fathom" the pathology of the disease more completely, neurologist Dr. John Donley published an article entitled "On Neurasthenia as a Disintegration of Personality" in the *Journal of Abnormal Psychology* in 1906 (55). In the article, he argued for a single cause of the multitudinous symptoms and manifestations of nervousness, one that was rooted in the patient's sense of him or herself as master of both the self and the environment:

> The fundamental mood produced by the pleasurable flow of the organic
> sensations is one of freedom, energy, comfort. . . . On the other hand, any
> disturbance of these organic sensations will result in feelings of anxiety,

fear, helplessness, and discomfort. Filled as we assume with the feeling of well-being,—a normal inner life,—our . . . [subject] finds that when he approaches his environment, the outer life of relation, he is able to adapt himself to it with facility, both because of his subjective stability, and because this environment in the ideas, sensations, and emotions which it evokes is agreeable, making no demands which he is not able to supply. (59)

Neurasthenia emerges, according to Donley, when the outer environment demands a level of adaptability and flexibility that a personality is not able to accommodate or manipulate, when changes in the social world challenge one's inner sense of "comfort, stability, and power" (58). In other words, when the White personality does not experience the ease, comfort, and power that it has come to expect and upon which it relies, it experiences a crisis, a disintegration of personality. While Donley's understanding of the underlying cause of neurasthenia seems not to have fundamentally shifted contemporary medical approaches to the disease, it is noteworthy for the implicit and certainly unintended commentary it makes on the psychology of the White elite in the early years of the twentieth century. To assert that neurasthenia is the "problem of personality in a state of disintegration" was no small matter (57). It suggested that elite whites suffered psychological disease and disability (which I read as "dis-ease" and "dis-ability") that rendered them unable to function in the modern world.

Beard's conception of neurasthenia became dogma, though, and his success in popularizing neurasthenia as a medical diagnosis and cultural discourse that explained a wide range of anxieties and complaints among White Americans is evidenced by the number of other cultural workers who used it as a frame for their work. While the symptoms may have been disparate, dozens of early-twentieth-century artists, intellectuals, politicians, and "common folk," both real and imagined, suffered from neurasthenia. What they seemed to share, however, was a sense of being thrown off balance by the personal and social possibilities emerging for the future. With one foot in the Victorian era, with its clearly delineated values and behavioral expectations, and the other in the transitional modern era, where these norms were routinely being challenged, sufferers of nervousness often experienced a divided sense of self or a personality at war with itself. The surety they once experienced as the White elite undermined by rapid social change, they found themselves unsure of how to understand or constitute themselves in the modern world. Neurasthenia gave a conceptual name and frame for their distress and then normalized it such that it was no longer a cause for the nation's concern. It became the means for defining and identifying the White cultural elite.

This sense of being both fit and unfit, which results in a "wasting of energies," is what leads Henry Wonham to characterize White double consciousness as an instantiation of neurasthenia. However, Du Bois was clearly not satisfied that this divided consciousness was located in or could be resolved by medicine or psychology. Rather, Du Bois offered a *sociological* reading of the origins and implications of White double consciousness, arguing that it was largely the result of a particular history of interracial contact in the United States and particular choices that White Americans were making about how to constitute their racial identities. He sought to shift the terms of the conversation about White double consciousness so that White supremacist thinking would be understood not as the standard of White mental health, but as an irrational nervous disorder that sapped the energy and talents of the nation.

Race relations in United States had been deteriorating for over a decade by the time Du Bois was completing his studies at Harvard in the late 1800s. On the heels of an abandoned Southern Reconstruction program, White violence and terror increased exponentially as White people in the South reasserted their economic, political, and social domination of African Americans. Racist repression was at the heart of the convict labor system that criminalized and then effectively reenslaved Black bodies,[7] and in the array of Jim Crow laws that governed, with threat of violence, the social behavior of African Americans and interracial interactions between whites and blacks. The rise of the Ku Klux Klan as an extralegal, sanctioned force of White oppression had the potential to affect just about all areas of African American action, from the pursuit of education to the exercise of political rights, and race riots became a common occurrence in cities throughout the South. In the North, recently emancipated Black workers were in competition with unskilled white laborers, increasing racial tensions in that region also. All of the violent confrontations and acts of social domination that characterized the mid- to late nineteenth century lead Herbert Shapiro, author of *White Violence and Black Response: From Reconstruction to Montgomery*, to conclude that in the years following Reconstruction, America (and especially the South) was locked in "a kind of informal civil war" for the heart of the nation. "Acts of terror in the South" he continues, "challenged the federal government to demonstrate its willingness to enforce constitutional rights, and the government's response was to show that it would not take the action necessary to suppress racist violence" (8).

Du Bois himself would produce a seminal study of the Reconstruction era entitled *Black Reconstruction in America, 1860–1880* later in his career. Rather than focus on the violence of the period, however, he provided a Marxist analysis that examined the ways in which race was used to divide black and white workers to prevent exploited people from uniting to improve their economic conditions. He theorized why a nation that had fought to realize the democratic principles of equality would turn once again "to embrace and worship the color bar as social salvation" when it had done nothing but foster "mutual hatred and contempt, at the summons of a cheap and false myth" (723). He also called attention to the "psychological difficulties of the planters" who "tried to hide" from the affronts that slavery made to their moral sensibilities (43). By 1935, when *Black Reconstruction* was published, Du Bois had been at the forefront of the struggle for Black civil rights for more than three decades, yet he never abandoned his critique of White double consciousness as the foundation for much of America's racial strife. In the early 1900s, however, he was in the early stages of exploring the connection between racism and America's mental and social health.

"White double consciousness," however, is not a term that Du Bois used. While much of his work pointed toward his interest in white psychology and identity, double consciousness was a term he reclaimed and reserved to explain the peculiar and painful plight of African-descended people in the West. In challenging contemporary understandings of neurasthenia as an exclusively white disease, Du Bois made several critical moves. First, by demonstrating that racism created in African Americans the same psychological discontinuities that medical researchers claimed modern advances produced in white Americans, he argued that elite White Americans were not the only ones who could experience a "wasting of energies" that had significant effect on them and the society. In rewriting the Black experience as quintessentially American, his articulation of (black) double consciousness intersects and enters a rhetorical dialogue with the cultural discourse of neurasthenia. In this intervention, Du Bois stresses the "dogged strength" of the Negro soul, a pointed allusion to the fragile psychological and physical state of White America that was acknowledged in the discourse of neurasthenia (365). In drawing attention to the contrast between white fragility and black strength, he calls into question whether white elites should have exclusive control over shaping the future of America. Second, in the moment when Du Bois "appropriate[s] nervous disease as African American cultural property," he fundamentally redefines the national and international conversation about modernity so that it includes social issues like the construction of race and gender, thereby integrating African Americans explicitly, and people of color more broadly, into any vision of the future (Wonham, 129). In effect, his concept of (black) double consciousness inscribes Blackness into psychology and history, but it is a subjectivity that emerges with clarity only when it assumes the power of the gaze and critiques the oppressive structures that have excluded it from both.

Double consciousness, then, was a part of the cultural exchange surrounding neurasthenia. Du Bois understood that science and medicine could be (and were being) appropriated by a state apparatus to legitimate and rationalize racism at all levels of society. What he saw as sociopolitical choices that enabled political inequality and the continued disenfranchisement of African American citizens, scientists were casting as biological inevitability. Stephen Jay Gould argues in *The Mismeasure of Man* that arguments for biological determinism, "the notion that people at the bottom are constructed of intrinsically inferior material (poor brains, bad genes, or whatever)," are "latecomers" to the social scene (63). The caution he offers in thinking about the role of science in this "debate" is one that Du Bois arrived at almost a century earlier. Gould writes, "white leaders of the Western nations did not question the propriety of racial ranking during the eighteenth and nineteenth centuries. In this context, the pervasive assent given by scientists to conventional rankings arose from shared social belief, not from objective data gathered to test an open question" (66). Gould, of course, would demonstrate that the work of many of the country's most respected nineteenth-century scientists was unconsciously distorted by their a priori belief in White racial superiority. And while the "prevalence of *unconscious* finagling" leads Gould to conclude that the "social context of science" is much more important than we typically acknowledge, the reality of scientific racism leads Du Bois to a different line of inquiry (87–88). The question becomes not *how* these distortions and misrepresentations happen so broadly in a society, but *why*, which leads Du Bois to try to fathom the psychology of Whiteness.

Perhaps the earliest suggestion of Du Bois's interest in *white* (double) consciousness and the course that his social and intellectual work would take is evidenced in the commencement address he delivered upon earning his bachelor's degree in history at Harvard University in 1890. In "Jefferson Davis as a Representative of Civilization," the newly degreed Du Bois confronted contemporary attempts to rewrite the history of the Civil War by celebrating Confederate officers and Southern politicians as heroic, noble patriots who fought valiantly for their principles. In the commencement address, Du Bois lambasted these efforts as misguided and destructive, a betrayal of history, human potential, and the truth. For him, Jefferson Davis "was a typical Teutonic hero," a man who, without regard for the larger implications of his actions or arguments, sought to "advance . . . [one] part of the world at the expense of the whole" ("Jefferson Davis," 811–812). Du Bois deftly painted Davis as an iconic example of the ethos of White America (and, more broadly, Western civilization) and an ideology that justified one group exercising near-complete power over another simply because it could. This was, for the young intellectual, individualism in the extreme, "the overweening sense of the I and the consequent forgetting of the Thou" (812). Rather than protecting the weakest members of the society, this ideology justified their exploitation and oppression; rather than seeking to elevate the least advanced human communities, this doctrine celebrated "the Strong Man crushing out an effete civilization" (812). Lamenting the direction in which America and all of Western civilization was drifting, Du Bois argued to his audience, "Judged by the whole standard of Teutonic civilization, there is something noble in the figure of Jefferson Davis; and judged by every canon of human justice, there is something fundamentally incomplete about th[e] standard" (811).

Jefferson Davis, with his "nervous lips and flashing eye," was for Du Bois not only a study in contrasts but also a study of how selective memory and historical distortion were being deployed by White America to bolster White racial identity and psychology (811). Davis was being celebrated as a strong, heroic man in American historical and cultural discourse, but all mention of his brutality and regressive and divisive politics were being excised from his public image. In this way, Davis could become an exemplar of "Anglo-Saxon" culture: he was a soldier "who defied disease, trampled on precedent, would not be defeated, and never surrendered" (811). Divorced from any conversation about his politics and the ideology to which he devoted his efforts, Davis (and other Confederate leaders) was being transmogrified by historians[8] into the defiant and indomitable American spirit, a man who represented the best of the "Strong Man" ideal. In this guise, his ambition and recklessness were touted as commitment, his brutality rewritten as military expertise. Du Bois saw these efforts at refashioning as charged attempts to recuperate a White self-image as the basis for postbellum national reconciliation. They allowed White Americans to ignore and deny the reality of Davis's life and legacy and the experience of African Americans in the United States. Thus, in his commencement address, Du Bois confronts the mythicization of Jefferson Davis, and as he corrects the historical record his subject reemerges as a "champion of a people fighting to be free in order that another people should not be free" (811). Honoring him as a Southern-turned-American hero becomes the commitment of a whole nation to an ideology of repression and division.

By 1903, when Du Bois published *The Souls of Black Folk*, the facts of slavery and Reconstruction had been distorted so completely that few white Americans were taught that the Civil War was anything other than a mistake. The fight for freedom for all human beings and the attempt to live up to the promise of the democratic ideals of the Constitution were routinely disparaged as a misguided liberalism that actually undermined liberty rather than advanced it. Additionally, as Du Bois had feared and predicted, the United States was continuing to retreat from full political and social participation of the country's African American citizens; instead, White violence and repression of African Americans in all facets of American life were escalating. Du Bois biographer David Levering Lewis points out that at the time of Du Bois's writing, African Americans

> were being lynched in the South and ghettoized in the North, but there now loomed the even more horrendous prospect that such brutalities could cease to be deplored (however formally or hypocritically) as un-American and become, in the regime of the emergent ideology, officially sanctioned instruments of racial subjugation. (276)

The Souls of Black Folk was intended to intervene in the politics of repression and denial that was strangling any hope of racial equality, reconciliation, and progress. Hoping to capture the painful but heroic lives of Southern blacks and to chronicle the contributions of his people to an ungrateful nation, Du Bois offered a history and analysis of Southern race relations and their impact on millions of socioeconomically and educationally impoverished African Americans.

Yet the suffering and beauty of African American people and culture were not Du Bois's only subjects. There is much to suggest that even in this seminal text of African American psychology and sociology, Du Bois extended his earlier interest in White identity and consciousness. In chapters like "Of the Sons of Master and Man" and "Of the Coming of John," he confronts the ignorance, hypocrisy, and cowardice of White Southerners, carefully outlining how the social realities of Southern communities retard racial reconciliation and inflame prejudice on both sides of the color line. He begins his analysis of White identity by noting that "the characteristic of our age is the contact of European civilization with the world's underdeveloped peoples," the result of which has been "war, murder, slavery, extermination, and debauchery" (475). In considering these violent and oppressive cultural clashes, Du Bois argues for the need to examine "race-contact" in the United States as a means of understanding the tendency of White cultures to "put a premium on greed and impudence and cruelty" (476). Thus, in "Of the Sons of Master and Man," a chapter that promises to analyze not the past, but the present and future of America vis-à-vis a consideration of the *sons* of masters and men, Du Bois begins by leveling a sharp judgment against contemporary performances of Whiteness. For him, as his nuanced title indicates, to be a master is not to be a man; it makes one something other, something less than fully human. Whiteness denies cross-racial recognition and connection in favor of "brute force and cunning" (475). It is, as he had argued in "Jefferson Davis as a Representative of Civilization," the "overweening sense of the I and the consequent forgetting of the Thou."

Du Bois goes on to highlight the mechanisms by which White supremacy and prejudice are maintained in the South. In all facets of racial contact, he says, progress is inhibited by the color line such that "there is almost no community or intellectual life or point of transference where the thoughts and feelings of one race can come into direct contact and sympathy" with the other (488–489). This separation enables the continued subjugation of African Americans by strengthening the capacity of Whites to deny the humanity and shared aspirations of Black Americans. Du Bois makes this point poignantly in the chapter "Of the Coming of John," in which the paths of two Johns, one White and the other Black, cross tragically in the South. One John is sent to college, where he comes to recognize "the Veil that lay between him and the White world"; the other is educated in an institution that fails to challenge or disrupt his racial prejudices (525). The mother of the Black John is told that educating him "will spoil him" by the same family who sends their White John to Princeton to become a man (523). The two communities are united by a shared dream of education and advancement, yet Du Bois is careful to demonstrate that "neither world thought of the other world's thought, save with a vague unrest" (523). The unrest of the Black community is a desire for social acceptance and equality. The unrest of the White community, concomitantly, is a fevered attempt to deny the hypocrisy that defines their lives, to ignore the humanity of their victims.

According to Du Bois, however, the recognition of black humanity was difficult to avoid. In an article entitled "Nigger and Knowledge: White Double-Consciousness in *Adventures of Huckleberry Finn*," Rhett S. Jones similarly argues that the humanity of African Americans was really never in question among White Americans, that "despite . . . public 'proofs' repeatedly and often presented by powerful men in every walk of life, most Whites were not able to escape knowledge of Black humanity" (175). The myriad personal and social rationales—religious, scientific, sociological, and economic—that were pressed into service to make the case for African American inferiority, then, were all mechanisms designed to protect a fragile White ego and society. The very pervasive and expansive presence of these discourses in nineteenth- and early-twentieth-century American society evidences the denial and repression necessary to sustain the myth of White supremacy. Du Bois captures this psychological dynamic in his presentation of the White John. While awaiting entry to a musical performance, he (the White John) describes to his companion the close and affectionate relationship he had with "a little Negro named after me," as a way of explaining the daily "cordial and intimate relations between White and Black" that exist in the South (*Souls of Black Folk*, 526). When, only moments later, he finds himself seated next to an African American man, however, he is indignant and "flush[es] to the roots of his hair" before "he hesitated and grew pale with anger, called the usher and . . . with a few peremptory words . . . slowly sat down" (526). What Du Bois reveals in these few sentences is the fantasy of cross-racial connection that Whiteness has chosen to embrace as reality. The White John is far from comfortable with people of color; in his community, the barriers to cross-racial recognition and intimacy are formidable. He is expected to get only so close to people of color, and to maintain the proper attitude of superiority even then. Thus, while he certainly is invested in believing that "cordial and intimate relations" between Whites and Blacks are commonplace, the Africanist presence John has conjured becomes unstable in the presence of an actual African American person. He immediately becomes hyperaware of and hypersensitive to the racial Other, who, by his very presence, challenges John's construction of reality. He is forced to confront his own self-serving delusion of racial harmony in the South, and to face the tenuous and ultimately unsustainable nature of his fantasy. At the very moment that he speaks to an usher to demand the removal of the offending Black body, readers are made aware of the violence that is necessary to maintain his sense of himself and his world.

Ironically, though, the White John (and, by extension, the White community) must acknowledge on some deeply repressed level the humanity of the Black bystander exactly *because* of this fantasy of racial intimacy: only subjects can establish such connection with each other. Thus, John must recognize the subjectivity of African Americans even as the ideology of White supremacy that he has embraced demands that he deny it. Diane Harriford and Becky Thompson, authors of the essay "Secrets," also speak to the situation Du Bois dramatizes in this chapter of *Souls*, the schizophrenic contradictions of race relations in the historical South. They write, "Consciously, white people have to keep black people away from them. Unconsciously, they want black people back—their sisters, their nannies, their playmates. They want the family back. They want their kin back" (n.p.). That is exactly where the White John finds himself, longing for a connection—missing someone who is like family to him—while simultaneously unable to acknowledge or act on his desire. His mind is thrown out of balance in this moment of confrontation, and his subconscious must work quickly to right itself. He cannot avoid or contain the psychological discord that an African American person looses in him, thus he resorts to more conscious and extreme expressions of power to calm his disquiet and assert his will for how things should be.

In his representation of the actions and reactions of the White John, Du Bois seems clearly to be drawing on nineteenth-century understandings of mental stability and reason. Thomas Cooley has thoroughly researched Victorian concepts of the healthy and diseased body and the connection of those concepts to their understandings of race and gender. In *The Ivory Leg in the Ebony Cabinet*, he presents a picture of a scientific community that was obsessively concerned with the examination, cataloging, and measurement of the human body. Of particular interest to this discussion are Victorian understandings of the physical construction of the brain and metaphorical conceptions of the mind. The brain was believed to be divided into distinct units, or faculties, that controlled thought, reasoning, and personality. Cooley finds that before 1909, when Sigmund Freud lectured in the United States, "the median American mind harbored no recognizably modern notion of the unconscious" (2). Sanity was defined as the parts of the brain working harmoniously, with none of the parts dominating the others. Mental disorder, on the other hand, was conceived of as a mind "cut off" or "divided from itself," a disassociation of the mind's constituent parts (29). Cooley goes on to explain that the test for insanity was twofold. One was believed to be insane when one demonstrated a "perversion of the emotions and passions" that was not based in reason and/or reality *and* when that disconnect from reality "took possession" of the victim rather than the "madma[n] taking hold of his obsession" (Skae quoted in Cooley, 30, 41). In other words, the expectation was *not* that people did not have insane thoughts, but rather that they would work to banish those fantasies rather than act on them. The assertion of self-control in the face of periodic psychological instability marked one as sane; the embrace of the perverted reality was the surest sign of insanity. These were the theories that Du Bois would have learned even as concepts of the (healthy) mind were beginning to change.

According to this framework of mental health, the White John was not stable. He was driven mad by racism, a condition that Du Bois believed was increasing throughout America. John exhibited a dis-integrated, "ill-harmonized" mind that was unable to distinguish between reality and fantasy, one for which the delusion of White superiority served as the real (Du Bois, *Souls of Black Folk*, 545). Certainly logic suggests that this prevailing definition of insanity should have been a powerful challenge to the discourse of neurasthenia in particular, and to the arguments of scientific racism more generally. In drawing on this discourse of the constitution of the mind, Du Bois asserts that the responses of White Americans to issues of race were the obsessive reactions of a mind at war with itself (i.e., its moral and intellectual "faculties" are disassociated) and out of touch with reality. He creates a space in which racism can be understood as an irrational response to a delusional sense of reality. In this context, John's struggles to acquire psychological balance once again are significant: his primary mechanism for doing so is to embrace his irrational and illegitimate understanding of the world. He becomes more adept at self-deception, less able to reason or understand, and more willing to violently assert his construction of the world.

This engagement with the scientific seems only a point of entry for Du Bois, however, for very quickly it becomes clear that John's actions are located in the social and historical realms—in his sense of himself as a White man and all that that means during this time—and not in the faulty workings of a diseased mind. John makes conscious choices about which strategies he will use to resolve the conflicts he experiences between his idealized self-conception and fantasy of a racially harmonious South and the contested reality that is forced upon him by the presence of African American people. These *choices*, ultimately, are the place where Du Bois locates White identity and psychology. When the author has the men recognize each other (the African American man seated next to the White John is the John of his childhood reminiscences), this moment of recognition is a catalyst for yet another crisis for Whiteness; the social conditions that Du Bois has previously described as fueling the development of double consciousness in African Americans are shown to be at work for White subjectivity also. The White John, here, is stuck between two gazes: that of his Northern, white, female companion and that of his childhood friend. The two racial performances required in this moment are at odds with one another. Du Bois writes, "The White John started, lifted his hand, and then froze into his chair" (527). While it does not excuse the role he played in having the then-unknown African American Other removed from the theater, it is notable that John's instinct is to intervene on behalf of someone he knows; his unmediated response is to connect. In failing to do so he allows racial conventions to overwhelm his recognition of and connection to another human being. He is forced once again to confront his hypocrisy and, additionally in this case, his lack of freedom and courage to act as he would choose. He is forced to contemplate, as a different character does in William Kelly's *A Different Drummer*, "What if I hadn't done something that perhaps I should have done? Suppose I was a coward when I should, when I COULD have been brave? . . . I'm a coward when I don't have to be" (143). All of these character lapses, doubts, and moral failures are witnessed by the Black John, who "smiled lightly, then grimly" (*Souls of Black Folk*, 527).

John's silence in the theater is usefully juxtaposed to the later vocal performance he enacts when his father tells him that his childhood playmate has also returned to the community. Upon hearing this information, "the young man's face flushed angrily, and then he laughed . . . it's the darky that tried to force himself into a seat beside the lady I was escorting—" (533). John's unconscious affect suggests his continuing discomfort with the image of himself that he has been forced to confront. He cannot forget his mendacity and moral lapses, nor does he have the courage to become the man he believed himself to be. He has not only been seen by the Other, but has now seen himself and knows himself to be flawed, weak, and as circumscribed by social convention as those whom he racially dominates.

The flush of his skin that seven years earlier had signaled his reluctant confrontation with his own self-deception and self-alienation is now an indication of his shame and self-serving refusal to reject the dissimulation of his society. Instead of using his discomfort to fuel personal growth and honesty, he retreats to anger and a deeper entrenchment in lies that support his status as a White man. He fabricates an encounter with his African American counterpart that he knows will enrage his father (who is a judge and powerful man in the community), representing the Black John as an aggressive social interloper whose crime is not only his intrusion upon "White" space and society but also his fully human and sexual presence. However, in regurgitating the myth of the Black male threat, John implicitly acknowledges the possibility of interracial desire and sexual competition—which, at heart, is the recognition of the Black John's humanity. Claiming exclusive right to the White female body is not an assertion of power. Rather, it evidences his anxiety over social changes that muddy the distinctions between White and Black male bodies, and his continuing inability to escape and unwillingness to resolve his White double consciousness. The Black John's deepest transgression is that he is a "disagreeable mirror" (to borrow James Baldwin's phrase) for Whiteness; he is vilified because his undeniable humanity refuses Whiteness an unsullied retreat into self-deception ("Guilt," 409).

In light of this psychological drama that Du Bois makes visible in the character of the White John, the segregation of lives that he describes in the chapter entitled "Of the Sons of Master and Man" is revealed to have a far more insidious and utilitarian function for Whiteness. The enforced physical and social separation of segregation allows White people "in their conversations with one another" to "make reassuring sounds" that mitigate or absolve them of responsibility for human suffering (Baldwin, "Guilt," 722). It allows them to believe in White moral and social superiority because the very bodies that would challenge those prejudices are socially degraded, excessively policed, and forcefully excluded. White double consciousness has a solid footing in fear—fear of being truly seen by an Other and fear of seeing oneself honestly. It is a mind divided against itself, feverishly erecting defenses to prevent true self-consciousness and the heavy responsibility of change and growth that often attend such self-awareness. The White psyche is troubled, Du Bois suggests, by divided aims: the one toward human recognition and connection, the other toward self-aggrandizement and selective advancement. This divided mind leads to an obsessive focus on the darker-skinned Other that often results in "the loss of self-control that was thought to enslave the human will in acute cases" (Cooley, 41). Thus, unlike much of the medical and psychological discourse of the time, *The Souls of Black Folk* strongly suggests that investment in White supremacist ideology makes one unfit for rule because it leads to ever more obsessive and unreasonable thoughts and behaviors.

To make this final point emphatically, Du Bois ends the "Coming of John" chapter with an overdetermined confrontation between the two protagonists. The White John, who has just lied to his father about his run-in with the Black John, suddenly is acutely restless. He "wander[s] aimlessly"; things seem "old and stale . . . [and] flat"; and he finally complains, "Good Lord! How long will this imprisonment last" (533–534). His choice of words is important. After race-baiting his father to action (the judge immediately uses his power to fire John and shut down the "Negro" school where John has been teaching), everything in his hometown of Altamaha seems anachronous, confining, and far too easy to manipulate. The White John is simultaneously agitated and bored, his "energies" having been wasted on a task that has not prevented him from coming face-to-face with his own moral weaknesses and social limitations. As he seeks to calm his disquiet, he notices Jennie, John's sister, and accosts her, an act so nonsensical that readers are invited to question his sanity once again. It is clearly not the action of a reasoned man whose mental faculties are working harmoniously. He is at once a petulant and impish child and a dangerous predator, acting purely from wildly swinging emotions: "'Hello, Jennie! Why you have n't kissed me since I came home,' he said gaily. The young girl stared at him in surprise and confusion . . . and attempted to pass. But a willful mood had seized the young idler, and he caught her arm. Frightened, she slipped by; and half mischievously he turned and ran after her through the tall pines" (534). Certainly his attempts at recomposing himself and reasserting his power have tremendous impact on African American men and women in the community, but one cannot help but notice how erratic this young gentleman of the South is. He is unfocused and undisciplined, and acts without honor or purpose. Facing a Blackness seeking to reconstitute itself in a new sociopolitical structure—a new modernity—the White John is woefully unprepared to do the same. "On the Coming of John" raises serious questions about the fitness of a neurasthenic white elite that would go to such ends to maintain such a contradictory fantasy of themselves and the world.

While Du Bois's early work sought to intervene in a cultural conversation about neurasthenia by carving a sociopolitical space for African American contributions to the future of the United States, *Souls of Black Folk* went much further than a simple direct attack on the premises and suppositions of that medical discourse. In reclaiming double consciousness as African American cultural property, Du Bois provided an early, critical scaffolding on which to examine the effect of racism on the souls of White folk. His intervention was initially located in medical discourse, questioning whether a possessive investment in Whiteness was evidence of, or a source of, White mental instability. But even early in his career, he rejected the idea that White double consciousness was a form of mental illness. Instead, with the eye of a historian and sociologist, Du Bois illuminated the cultural and historical causes of a white schizophrenic subjectivity, the day-to-day choices that precipitated a mind, and soul, at war with itself.

Born in 1858, Charles Chesnutt's childhood and early adulthood were shaped by the turbulent, hopeful, and ultimately disappointing years bracketed by the Civil War and post-Reconstruction era. He was fair-skinned enough to pass for white, and his journals bristle with indignation, disillusionment, and frustration as he attempted to negotiate the indiscriminate nature of a racial caste system that not only actively worked against the advancement of an entire group of people but also failed to acknowledge natural intellect, talent, and refinement among that group simply because of their racial classification. He turned to writing as a means of redress and reform, declaring in a May 29, 1880, journal entry, "If I do write, I shall write for a purpose, a high, holy purpose. . . . The object of my writings would not be so much the elevation of the colored people as the elevation of the whites,—for I consider the unjust spirit of caste which is so insidious as to pervade a whole nation . . . a barrier to the moral progress of the American people" (*Journals*, 139–140). He believed that the best strategy for instigating social change around the issue of race lay in transforming the thinking and shifting the perspectives of white Americans. Chesnutt's novelistic efforts to "elevate" white Americans took two complementary directions. On the one hand, his goal led him to create black characters who encouraged white readers to engage empathetically with African American lives. Chesnutt utilized this approach in his first two published novels, *The House Behind the Cedars* and *The Marrow of Tradition*. These texts focus on fair-skinned African American characters, demonstrating their ability to be as successful and cultured as whites if not prevented by racial prejudices, prohibitions, and socially imposed limitations to their education and aspirations. The tragedy in each novel is precipitated by the social codes and norms that bar blacks from fully participating in and contributing to American culture, which is understood to be exclusively "White." A second approach Chesnutt used for bringing about a moral revolution in white America was to present Whiteness "with the veil withdrawn," as Lydia Maria Child phrases it in her introduction to Harriet Jacobs's *Incidents in the Life of a Slave Girl*, to defamiliarize and denaturalize Whiteness so that white readers would have the opportunity to see themselves through an oppositional gaze (Child, 6). Chesnutt adopted this latter strategy in his only published white life novel, *The Colonel's Dream*, but white readers were not receptive to his sharp but well-intentioned critiques. While some critics and reviewers of his time commended *Dream* for being well written, realistic, and compelling, at least as many judged the novel as a sprawling, didactic treatise on the ills of the South "thinly disguised as a novel" ("Shattered Arcadia," 92). It did not sell well and was soon out of print.

The Colonel's Dream centers on Colonel Henry French, a White Southerner by birth and former Confederate officer who has lived most of his postwar adult life in the northeast as a businessman. He returns to his hometown, Clarendon, after a twenty-year absence to find that little has outwardly changed about the town. The community seems a bit older and more worn, but the values and ways of moving in the world, which French appreciates and largely wants to see preserved, are intact. Yet Colonel French is also a study in contrasts, a man with a foot in two worlds. There are elements of Clarendon's "charm" that disturb him: the overtly racist attitudes that many of its White citizens hold, which, as a Northern capitalist, he sees as antiquated and irrelevant; the lack of industry, employment, and economic progress in the town; and the blatant acts of discrimination and injustice that he witnesses. Believing himself to be a pragmatic problem solver, he sets in motion several large-scale community improvement projects designed to get whites and blacks working, confident that the former group will relinquish their racist ideologies and actions once their economic situations improve. But he is easily persuaded to scale back his plans to avoid offending and alienating the local White population. Ultimately he is thwarted and driven out of Clarendon before any of his projects, or his vision, can be realized.

The colonel, as he is known, is torn between his desire for a nostalgic return to plantation culture in the South and his vision of a more prosperous and egalitarian "New South."⁹ The region appeals to him because its conservative social values around race and gender remain intact, yet he is shaken by the overt and cruel ways in which that power is maintained, especially over African Americans. Colonel French would prefer a benevolent, "gentle" rule, such as the one he romantically imagines existed before the Civil War, the one he believes his family exercised during their reign as White elites in Clarendon. Yet, at moments when he honestly evaluates the past, he recognizes that the exercise of power in the antebellum South was inhuman and that he, as a member of the propertied class, could choose to engage that reality at his discretion. French's ability to know, and "not know," the cost of his privilege makes him a perfect subject in which to explore Chesnutt's intervention in the cultural conversations surrounding White double consciousness. Chesnutt's analysis echoes that of Du Bois in significant ways, including his representation of neurasthenia as personal and social debilitation. However, where Du Bois saw white double consciousness arising from an unwillingness to confront the black gaze that could pave the way for a truer self-consciousness within Whiteness, Chesnutt suggests that the "condition" can also result from Whiteness's reluctance to judge its own past and refusal to act on that knowledge to chart a path for the future.

When we first meet Mr. French, as he is known in the North where he has spent the past twenty years of his life, he is in his New York office with one of his partners awaiting news of whether their business has sold. The office is alive with the accoutrements of a new, modern era: electric clocks and watches tick, telephones are poised to ring, and push buttons stand ready to summon immediate assistance. French, a middle-aged man whose life has straddled two eras, seems also to have become automated, nodding "mechanically" to the countdown his partner intones (6). Yet, juxtaposed to the breathlessly tense scene of mechanization and waiting is a physical description of French that establishes him as would-be master of these modern demands. He is tall and erect with an "unconscious ease," "firm chin," and "deep-set gray eyes" (5–6). We are told that he is an astute businessman who "fought for position" in the market when it became clear that the introduction of significant competition would eventually ruin his company, but we are also invited to read him as a good man, as his "spacious forehead" and "sensitive mouth" suggest his thoughtfulness, generosity, and big heart (6). French may be the picture of austere self-control, poised under extreme pressure and calm when others are agitated, but he is also a man with "a capacity for deep feeling" who is "more likely to be misled by the heart than by the head" (6). He seems to be modeled on a type of hero familiar in early-twentieth-century American fiction, following the path of literary reformers like Comfort Servosse in Albion Tourgée's *A Fool's Errand* and John March of George Washington Cable's *John March, Southerner.* Henry French is an exemplary specimen of the White, Northern, progressive capitalist—a level-headed businessman less concerned with race than with profit, a sensitive soul moved more by conviction than convention.

The omniscient narrator's glowing evaluation of the colonel is buttressed by a particular type of "evidence"—that of phrenology—that would have been familiar to early-twentieth-century readers. This pseudoscientific discourse held that differences in human biology, and particularly race, were indicative of internal capacities and aptitudes, were in effect *external markers* of an *internal and innate* superiority. As such, the descriptions of French's brow, chin, and posture are not simply incidental sketches of his physical appearance. In describing Colonel French's physical appearance in such detail, Chesnutt invokes a range of scientific arguments that spoke to a strictly biological rationale for human behavior and achievement in general, and White superiority in particular. This introduction suggested important elements of French's character, disposition, and fitness for leadership. It was a subtle but powerful subtext that supported the narrator's claims about the colonel and allowed white readers to think of him as a familiar and sympathetic character aligned with their understandings of themselves as moral, reasonable, and racially superior.

Yet Chesnutt constantly subverts his readers' expectations in this novel; little is as it appears. As Gary Scharnhorst points out in his essay "'The Growth of a Dozen Tendrils': The Polyglot Satire of Chesnutt's *The Colonel's Dream*," Chesnutt self-consciously draws from common genres, plots, and styles of his day only to rework them into a new and unfamiliar experience for his white readership. The same is true of his use of the scientific knowledge of his time. Colonel French is positioned in the first few pages as a fine and perhaps even representative example of empowered and self-possessed White masculinity. His external features bespeak his internal mental, emotional, and physical stability. However, when French finds that the sale of his business has been successful and he is richer than he has ever been, he promptly, and quite unexpectedly, faints.

French's neurasthenic collapse ushers in a moment of crisis for Whiteness in general, and White masculinity in particular. Even the stalwart and steady colonel is rattled by his brief loss of consciousness, commenting to his worried and attentive business partner, Mr. Kirby, "I . . . have fainted—like a woman," thereby aligning his physical condition with a more profound rereading of his unstable social status (8). The characters who attend to him reassure him that he is simply overworked and overstressed, but the unfolding plot suggests something more. At this juncture, Chesnutt introduces Mrs. Jerviss, French's widowed, third business partner. She has made her romantic interest in French plainly known, but he has not reciprocated her advances, choosing instead to focus on his work and his son. With the entry of Mrs. Jerviss into this convalescence scene, the colonel is cast even more emphatically into traditionally feminine roles. He is enfeebled and afflicted rather than strong and healthy, and is positioned as recipient, rather than bestower, of romantic attention. He represents a range of anxieties about the modern world, including those dealing with shifting gender roles and expectations about work, money, and urban life. His loss of consciousness and passive positioning in these scenes suggest that French's affliction is the result of more than stress and long workdays.

As I previously argued, the discourse of neurasthenia served many cultural functions in early-twentieth-century America. For the dominant society, it registered the anxiety that often accompanies large-scale cultural shifts and provided a language by which the physical and psychological effects of the rapidly changing modern era could be imagined and debated. By offering sufferers the means to "reexplain the world to themselves," it enabled patients, and society more broadly, to negotiate the meaning of the political, social, cultural, and economic changes that characterized the Gilded Age (Lutz, 23). Because of the multiple roles that the disease played, Lutz is correct to point out the malleability of neurasthenia, that it is "less an ideological formation . . . than a multiaccented story . . . necessarily read differently from different social positions" (15). However, for African American intellectuals like Chesnutt and Du Bois who were concerned with issues of race in America, there was a consistent vision of the danger of neurasthenia as a racialized medical discourse. Both pointed to the ways in which the cultural conversation about nervousness served to legitimate the continuation of White sociopolitical control in the United States. Not only did neurasthenia explicitly posit that elite Whites *should* shape America's future, it tacitly supported a climate of racial terrorism to maintain that exclusive privilege by positing Whites as superior by virtue of their "increased capacity for sorrow [and] love" as well as their more refined "sensitiveness" (Beard, 118, 31). Given that Beard's *American Nervousness* was marketed to a lay audience, these claims take on an added importance, for they assert that the neurasthenic was not only more susceptible to the stresses of social change and upheaval but also implicitly a kinder, gentler, more responsive soul. The claim to the legitimacy of White leadership and rule, then, was twofold, and the discourse of neurasthenia pardoned, if not completely elided, the racial violence and oppression that were being deployed to ensure Whiteness's continued dominance.

One such moment occurs when the colonel comes face-to-face with the convict-lease system that had reinstitutionalized a form of slavery in the South. When, back home in Clarendon, he sees a group of African American prisoners being led down the street and then sold, "the unconscious brutality of the proceeding grated harshly upon the colonel's nerves" (Chesnutt, *Dream*, 68). In this psychologically disjunctive moment, two Frenches, so to speak, battle for dominance—the one who remembered only the joys of living in the South, and the one who more clearly sees how those pleasures of White Southern living were maintained:

> He had remembered the pleasant things . . . and in the sifting process of
> a healthy memory he had forgotten the disagreeable things altogether. . . .
> Things Southern, as he had already reflected, lived long and died hard, and
> these things which he saw now in the clear light of day, were also of the
> South, and singularly suggestive of other things Southern which he had
> supposed outlawed and discarded long ago. (69)

The collision of romanticized past and more objectively viewed past (and present) is so jarring that it raises the possibility that the colonel will suffer another neurasthenic episode. Like White John in *Souls of Black Folk*, Colonel French refuses to examine his discomfort further, choosing rather to dismiss his unease by returning to a familiar racist script: the negro "looked like an habitual criminal . . . one of the idle and worthless Blacks with so many of whom the South was afflicted" (66). It is not until he sees his formerly enslaved childhood caretaker, Peter, being auctioned to pay a vagrancy fine that he becomes outraged and driven to action. In the instant he chooses to act, however, the colonel's concern is less about Peter and more about how Peter's debased life reflects on the French family who once owned him. He indignantly purchases Peter "for life" to get him out of the penal system and vows "to provide in some way for his declining years" (73). In other words, French *chooses* to privilege the racist narrative to condone the proceedings, although his psychological and physiological responses suggest that he is not completely comfortable with the scene, and he acts only when he has a personal stake, even though in so doing he essentially legitimates and financially supports the corrupt convict-lease system.[10] His intellectual and emotional responses conflict with one another, leading to actions that can be easily co-opted by the racist social structures of the South.

French's divided mind and his collapse, both described early in the text, precipitate a crisis not only in his self-image but also in Chesnutt's White readers, who have been invited to see themselves in the protagonist. French appears vulnerable in his weakness, and the characters around him seem unnerved by his sudden prostration. Dr. Moffatt is called to check on the ailing patient and pronounces "after a brief examination" that the colonel has "a fine constitution" and no bad habits. He concludes that French has simply "been burning the candle at both ends," has overexerted himself with worry and fatigue and is in need of rest (11). The diagnosis itself would have been familiar to Chesnutt's contemporary readers; the colonel has expended more energy than he has replenished and has experienced a neurasthenic episode as a result. However, Moffatt does more than just offer a medical explanation for the collapse. His diagnosis is geared toward reassuring French (and Chesnutt's readers) that his *constitution* is sound despite the fainting episode. The doctor essentially reaffirms French's social standing by his (Moffatt's) medical presence, effectively removing all doubts about his physical and mental fitness. The stature of the White American afflicted with nervousness was never compromised by the diagnosis, and both Du Bois and Chesnutt saw the ways that neurasthenia was being used to recuperate Whiteness from questions about its claim to superiority and cultural dominance. Having been reassured of his solid biological pedigree (i.e., his "constitution"), and therefore his fitness for leadership, readers are subtly prepared to trust the colonel's progressive humanitarianism once he returns south. Rhetorically, the disease served to ease fears and misgivings about the status of the White elite and their ability to lead America into its promising future—and to elide the fundamental "problem" of their age: the color line. Without this veneer, French's decisions and actions later in the book would have been open to questioning and doubt.

While Chesnutt highlights the ways in which neurasthenia serves to mask the reality of an uncertain and distressed White masculinity, the irony is that it is an imperfect cover; much about the colonel's unstable social position remains unresolved. First, the onset of French's neurasthenic episode is simultaneous with the sale of his business. As Lutz has pointed out, "Beard, Mitchell, and other neurologists argued that social mobility was a prime cause of neurasthenia" because it personalized and particularized many of the dramatic shifts that were happening more broadly in American society (20). In this instant, the colonel must confront, perhaps for the first time, the new direction that his social and personal lives are likely to take. He will no longer be defined by his ownership and management of a large company, master to laborers whose livelihoods depend on his business acumen and decision making. Instead, French is now being forced into the smaller, more passive role of accomplished former businessman whose toughest decision is not how to manage withering competition but where to vacation. For Whiteness, and particularly for a White Northern masculinity that during this period has been defined as alert, agile, and engaged, this new personal and social landscape is alarming. All that French has known of his adult life—position, respect, self-assurance, and confidence—have, in an instant, changed. Thus, while Moffatt's prescription of three months of rest somewhere warm and within reasonable travel distance was common, it actually works to highlight the liminal space the colonel now occupies, as the doctor's recommendation of "rest" was more often prescribed for women than men.[11]

The instability of French's social and gender positioning is also highlighted by the personal discomfort he has felt as a Southern transplant establishing himself in the North in the modern era. He is a man, it is revealed, who has not been at all comfortable living in "a land of women's clubs and women's claims"; he much prefers the "charming domestic, life of the old South" characterized by respectful and demure women who allow him to exercise his socially ascribed dominance over them and on behalf of them (Chesnutt, *Dream*, 69). Nor has he particularly relished the competitive nature of Northern capitalism, which "judged the tree by its fruit" rather than respecting the "good breeding" of a gentleman (39). He has had to fight for position in this new economy and climate, at first striving for "equality with those above, and, this attained, for a point of vantage to look down upon former equals," but still has nurtured a sense of entitlement that is predicated on "good blood" and family status (69). Although he has made the necessary shifts to successfully establish himself in the North, he has never been at ease with the performance of White masculinity required there. With the leisure that his sudden wealth and retirement from business have brought, and his weakened physical and emotional states, he now seems "out of place" in the North. The doctor sends him south to reconstitute himself.

Thus, it is significant that Moffatt rules out a number of locales before finally settling on the South as a suitable location for French's recovery, for this region adhered to a premodern sense of community and identity that seemed to align more fully with French's new social position. Du Bois writes in *Black Reconstruction in America, 1860–1880*, "All their [White Southerners'] ideas of gentility and education went back to the days of European privilege and caste" (34). Similarly, John Hope Franklin argues in *The Militant South, 1800–1861*, that the ethos of the South was built on European models of culture and community, where the "wildest dreams of the Southern settler involved his establishing himself as a country gentleman, living in noble splendor, receiving the services of his coterie of subordinates, and discharging the obligations that his 'high position' imposed on him" (63). In returning south, French is being directed to a space that, by virtue of its geographical placement and feudal aspirations, is both shielded from and resistant to the fast-paced change of the modern era. Because the early-twentieth-century South did not have a rigid work ethic tied to its ideas of social class standing or masculinity, it was the perfect location for French to negotiate a new attitude toward labor and leisure, one that was more befitting of his new socioeconomic position. Clarendon provides him, in short, with a stable platform from which he can establish a new identity. It is a geographical place that offers him a more expansive, and apparently noncontradictory, psychological space to reinvent himself.

This process of reconstitution, however, is by no means simple. It implies that French has choices about how he wants to position himself vis-à-vis the social order in which he moves. It also highlights the fact that there are multiple and sometimes contradictory standards for the performance of White masculinity, a fact that French becomes anxiously aware of as he spends more time in Clarendon. There he is confronted with racists who would deny African Americans basic human rights to ensure the continued sociocultural elevation of Whiteness and to reinforce their racial, if not economic, privilege. He also cavorts with a Southern elite who, while less virulently racist than many of their lower-class counterparts, still refuses to stand on any issue that might shift the politics of power at work in the community. Although the colonel's racial progressivism is at times hesitant and unsure, he finds himself a minority voice with little persuasive power even among his peers. His ultimate battle, though, is with a postbellum model of Whiteness who is unflinching and unapologetic about his willingness to exploit human beings for profit, Bill Fetters. Fetters represents capitalism unfettered; he uses all means and ideologies at his disposal, without deep investment in any of them, to gain power, position, and economic advantage over others. White supremacy is for him simply another tool for maintaining control over whites and blacks alike. His cool detachment from and manipulation of the power struggles unloosed in this changing socioeconomic climate are yet another model of White masculinity the colonel finds in the small community of Clarendon. Initially, however, the move south allows him some space to reclaim and reassert a seemingly homogenous and stable identity with which he is both familiar and comfortable. In registering his general dissatisfaction with Northern social structures, which is really a complaint about the embattled status of Whiteness as a social organizing principle, French returns almost unthinkingly to a neoconservative performance of Whiteness in which race, class, and gender demarcations bolster and define Whiteness. The traditional "soul" of Southern Whiteness has not been eradicated in French despite twenty years of performing his race differently.

An obvious example of this retreat to Whiteness occurs when the colonel discovers that his family home is owned by African Americans. Shortly after he arrives in Clarendon, he takes a walk with his son past the homestead and sees "a neatly dressed coloured girl" sitting in a chair on the "piazza . . . with an air of proprietorship" (Chesnutt, *Dream*, 24). His quickened step indicates that he is troubled, but he seems largely unaware of his unease. Later, the African American town barber, William Nichols, tells the colonel that he and his family are "livin' in the same house you wuz bawn in," offering the home as a point of commonality between them. While flattering the good taste and elegance evidenced in the home's spacious construction, the barber eventually concludes, "'ef I'd be'n bawn White I sho' would 'a' be'n a 'ristocrat" (81). His comment is revealing. It is an indication of the distance Nichols has traversed economically if not socially; the clear and multiple distinctions that had once separated an African American barber and the elite White class are now fewer. He owns a business in Clarendon, where the colonel's grandfather had once built structures to develop the town; he lives in the home once owned by the Frenches, and aspires to a status that is reserved for Whites only through custom and violence. With the exception of his race and the reality of White supremacy that has prevented African American social mobility and elevation, Nichols has come very close to being Colonel Henry French's peer.

The response that Nichols's comment elicits is also revealing of the colonel's deeply held, but unacknowledged, beliefs. This collapsing of distinctions between the aristocratic White class (as defined by lineage and superior heritage) and the nouveau riche, and in some ways between black and white, evidence a social transformation of the magnitude that, as we have seen, physicians credited as a trigger for neurasthenia. The changes greatly disturb Colonel French. Dean McWilliams argues in *Charles W. Chesnutt and the Fictions of Race*, "Henry French is a Southern aristocrat, a designation that, for French, denotes more than class affiliation . . . [it] has both social and moral implications" (167). Indeed, the colonel truly believes that "blood" and refinement make him a better man than those who have come to money and position through other means, precisely because he sees himself as a guardian of culture and society. He feels accountable for ensuring America's progress and promise as they are articulated in a particular historical moment, even when that responsibility runs counter to his personal beliefs. Here, the shifting mores of the modern era necessitate, according to an aristocratic creed, that he be open to a more racially progressive personal and social agenda, but clearly, like so many in the South, Colonel French still harbors fundamentally conservative racial beliefs. He realizes that the only tangible differences that remain between him and Nichols are race and history and the difference that both make for Nichols's social standing, but he refuses to embrace either the opportunities that have been opened to African Americans or the possibility of additional social shifts that would further democratize the South. Once he grasps the tremendous changes that have swept Clarendon such that middle-class African American families now occupy spaces once reserved for those of "honorable ancestry," he acts swiftly to reassert a White identity that was once exclusive and unencroachable (Chesnutt, *Dream*, 39). His one conscious thought as he impetuously offers to buy the house is, "It [the home] was hallowed by a hundred memories, and now!—" (82). Unable even to complete the thought that acknowledges the presence of a black family in his ancestral home, he forcefully negotiates to reacquire the home, thereby displacing the visible indicators of social change. He follows the purchase by "restor[ing], as far as possible, the interior as he remembered it in his childhood" and having an "old-time party" complete with period costumes and "a Black fiddler . . . play[ing] quadrilles and the Virginia Reel" (96, 98).

These acts work to reconstitute the space in which French came to understand his identity (and responsibility) as a Southern gentleman. The purchase allows him to reclaim his position as a White patriarch and guardian of Clarendon, and the party publicly reestablishes his investment in Whiteness. In commissioning an "old-time party—say such a party as my father would have given, or my grandfather," he establishes specific parameters and expectations for the celebration (97). His homage to the mythic "good old days" of the antebellum South reasserts the preeminence of Whiteness and, simultaneously, the "appropriate" roles of African Americans in the spaces of Whiteness—as servants and entertainers rather than peers and social equals. The ease with which the colonel returns to the racist thinking of his former years is significant given that Du Bois described White psychology and behavior in *Dusk of Dawn* as "unconscious nervous reflexes" toward questions of race (679). Clearly, the colonel is not a man who is a deliberate social conservative. He takes on those forces in Clarendon when he puts Black men to work beside White men, pays them equal wages, and promotes them to positions of management over less skilled white workers. He argues against the racism of the South with dinner guests who hold those positions and tries to improve the lives of all of the town's citizens by challenging Bill Fetters, the son of a former slave driver who is willing to exploit anyone for his own gain. Yet, in every action the colonel attempts, he is wracked by divided aims. He wants to create a diversified and progressive economy in Clarendon but does not want the town to lose its "Southern ways"; he is willing to see more racial equality in the community, but stops short of using his money to facilitate that goal when he is told that the White community will not support his attempts at integration; and he wants to unseat the Fetters family from their newly established prominence, but only to reinstate the "proper" aristocratic families, and ultimately himself, to power. In the hands of Chesnutt, White double consciousness becomes a schizophrenic contradiction of goals and aims. The actions of the beleaguered colonel French are an attempt to reaffirm, despite his experiences that suggest otherwise, that Whiteness is stable and that it remains dominant. A battle is being waged between French's pronounced ideals and his subconscious desires and beliefs. The colonel remains deeply committed to Whiteness as a way to make meaning of both himself and his world.

Chesnutt may begin the interrogation of the colonel's "possessive investment in whiteness" by engaging contemporary medical discourses on neurasthenia, but like Du Bois, he does not end his intervention there (Lipsitz, vii). Rather, *The Colonel's Dream* quickly expands in scope to consider a range of questions about the sociohistorical foundations of Colonel French's divided mind as well as the effect that this White schizo-phrenic subjectivity has on the larger society. The author is no longer con-tent simply to point out the problems that are caused for African American citizens by racism. He now is compelled to interrogate why these dam-aging and damning performances of Whiteness persist, and to examine the psychological cost to White Americans who are so afflicted. These broader concerns move Chesnutt to craft a narrative that defies readerly expectations for the successful White male protagonist, thereby prompt-ing that readership to consider where Southern patriarch and Northern industrialist Henry French has gone wrong.

One facet of the colonel that Chesnutt seems particularly critical of is his refusal to fully acknowledge the continuing effects of the South's racist past on the present. French acts as if the particular history of social stratifi-cation, injustice, and inequality in the South has not happened, which ren-ders him considerably less able to anticipate or counter the resistance to racial and economic transformation that he finds in Clarendon. He seems completely unable to understand, for instance, why Fetters would refuse to relinquish "ownership" of Bud Johnson. Johnson challenges Fetters's power and authority over him through his defiance and by escaping when possible. Fetters's agent explains, "He's defied our rules and defied the law, and defied me . . . and he ought to be made an example of. We want to keep 'im; he's a bad nigger, an' we've got to handle a lot of 'em, an' we need 'im for an example—he keeps us in trainin'" (*Dream*, 216). Thus, whenever Johnson is recaptured, Fetters pays the fine to reacquire him. Had Colonel French but considered more fully the ethos of the Southern White man who refuses to be bested by a "nigger" on pain of undermining his self-image and reputation in the community, Fetters's decision would not have been unfathomable to him and French might have been better able to find an effective strategy for intervention on Johnson's behalf. He would have also had a better chance of seeing how Fetters was using race to maintain allegiances and prevent cross-racial alliances that could have threatened his dominance in the community. And finally, the colonel would have at least marginally discerned how his actions, like buying "a dog, a house and a man," might support rather than subvert the racist social structure of the South, how his grandiose but solitary plans might be used by Fetters to maintain power in and over the community, or how the community's rac-ists might respond to his unsupported, one-man campaign for even mod-est social change (84). French clearly wants to operate as if the past has no continuing influence over the thinking or expectations of white folks in the South; his blindness impedes his efforts at social reform.

Closely related to the colonel's refusal to acknowledge the persistence of history in the present is his attendant refusal to fully acknowledge the wrongs of the past (and present). He has, as his Southern love interest Laura Treadwell observes, "learned new things without losing . . . [his] love for the old" (Chesnutt, *Dream*, 85). In choosing to continue to "love the old" and embrace the values of a community still pursuing White superiority as a social organizing principle, however, he denies the fundamental immorality of racism while simultaneously rejecting the turn toward democracy that society has taken. French wants to operate as if he can be both a progressive Northern capitalist *and* a Southern gentleman, as if the two value systems and the two performances of White masculinity somehow can be merged. He attempts this psychological and social balancing act, as we have previously seen, by turning to the rhetoric of biological determinism to explain racial inequities and abuses rather than acknowledging the injustices of Whiteness. While able to see that the only "convicts" being caught up in the convict-lease system are African Americans, he still justifies the proceedings by noting that many looked like "habitual criminal[s]" (66). Similarly, he implicitly acknowledges the privilege and economic boon Whiteness received from the institution of human bondage when he muses, "Had Peter remained a slave, then the colonel would have remained a master, which was only another form of slavery." Yet he turns around only minutes later to conclude, "Peter had returned home poor and broken . . . *because nature first*, and society next, in distributing their gifts, had been niggardly with old Peter" (31–32; emphasis mine). Scientific racism becomes a convenient cover for ignoring the evidence of White inhumanity and social domination, effectively blaming "nature" for Peter's condition.

Chesnutt seems intent on stripping away all of the psychosocial defenses the colonel and his white counterparts (and readers) enlist to shield them from the knowledge of the continuing legacies of race and history in the present. In one of the unwieldy but important subplots of *The Colonel's Dream*, Chesnutt exposes the unresolved trauma of history and explores the need for Whiteness to face its own responsibility for the suffering of others. In the story line, Malcolm Dudley has spent most of his adult life regretting and paying for an impetuous decision he made as a young man. Dudley, we learn, was a bachelor and manager of his uncle's estate. He had taken an enslaved woman, Viney, as his mistress, and they, along with the field hands and one other house slave, occupied the estate for more than ten years. Dudley decides to propose to a wealthy widow to help secure his future and to return his family to its former prominence, effectively displacing Viney as mistress of the home. When he announces his intention to marry, Viney speaks to the widow, causing the latter to end the engagement. Furious over Viney's actions, Dudley instructs the overseer to whip her and leaves the premises while his orders are executed. He discovers shortly thereafter that his uncle had come to the home and hidden money on the property; Viney is the only person who knows where the money was hidden, but she claims to be unable to speak as a result of her beating. Dudley spends the remainder of his long life caring for Viney in hope that she will regain her voice so that she can reveal her secret, all the while digging holes throughout the property looking for the money his uncle left, a fortune that would reestablish his family's name and position in the community. When Dudley is dying, Viney reveals that she never lost her ability to speak and that he has wasted his whole life looking for gold that does not in fact exist. She explains at long last, "He came . . . and left the gold. . . . An hour later *he came back and took it all away.* . . . The money was here one hour, but in that hour you had me whipped. . . . I have had my revenge! For twenty-five years I have watched you look for—nothing; have seen you waste your time, your property, your life, your mind—for nothing!" (287). Dudley exercised his prerogative as a White man in taking an enslaved woman as his mistress and in having her beaten at his will. For the remainder of his life he gently cares and provides for the woman whose body and affections he had previously assumed his for the taking by virtue of his race and position. He certainly regrets what his actions have cost him and, from the time that Viney falls mute, performs his Whiteness quite differently.

Chesnutt uses this poignant moment of confrontation, revenge, and regret as an example of the ways that the ghosts of the past haunt the present. Dudley has spent a lifetime paying for a decision made in haste and anger, but despite his actions after that fateful day, he never makes amends to the woman he has wronged. Viney has not forgiven him, and he is unable to forget what his betrayal and cruelty have cost him—money, security, and status among his peers. However, it seems that the source of his failure is not solely located in the calculated nature of his apology or in any insincerity, but in his *refusal* to honestly engage Viney's pain or his responsibility for it. He continues to apologize for ordering her to be whipped, but he simply ignores the suggestive comment the doctor makes when he examines the victim: "The woman has had a stroke . . . brought on by brutal treatment." When the chagrined Dudley assures the doctor that the overseer will be dismissed, the doctor replies, "You had better shoot him. . . . He has no soul—and what is worse, no discrimination" (175). Based on arguments about interracial sexual desire that were advanced during this time, the doctor's comment implies that the White overseer had debased himself by having sex with a black woman. It is a not-so-subtle suggestion that Viney has been raped in addition to being beaten. Yet the only acknowledgement of this possibility that Dudley makes is to tell Viney, "Martin went further than I intended, and I have discharged him for his brutality" (176). His curt denial, however, precludes Viney from speaking the totality of her victimization. It is not until Dudley is dying that she is able to articulate, albeit with typical Victorian decorum, her pain:

> "You had me whipped," she said. "Do you remember that? You had me whipped—whipped—whipped—by a poor White dog I had despised and spurned! You had said that you loved me, and you had promised to free me—and you had me whipped! . . . Mars' Ma'colm, you had me whipped—*by another man!*" (286)

Dudley's crime is his betrayal; the beating he sanctioned is only a symptom of this much deeper hurt he caused Viney. He discarded her affection when he sought a (white) wife, denied her humanity when he failed to grant her freedom, and injured her even further by exposing her to physical and sexual violation at the hands of a man she had already rejected. Yet, for all of the torment he has caused Viney, he apologizes only for his last decision, without acknowledging the rape even then. Dudley's marginal and self-serving engagement with Viney's humanity should be a stunning example of a self-imposed ignorance and refusal to accept responsibility for the full extent of the pain he has caused this African American woman. Unfortunately, though, it is merely representative of the decisions that Whiteness makes daily to deny and disregard the suffering that African Americans have endured at its hands. It is a history that has corrupted and infected every facet of present-day America, a history that has not died, but been denied. Both Viney and Dudley play out in the present a script that was started in the past, unable to liberate themselves from their traumatic history (which is, itself, a metaphor for the national legacy of slavery) because it is largely unclaimed and unspoken.

By defamiliarizing and demythologizing Whiteness, Du Bois and Chesnutt make critical interventions that they hoped would enable white readers to see themselves more objectively and honestly. In the thirty or so years that elapsed between Southern Reconstruction and the publication of *The Souls of Black Folk* and *The Colonel's Dream*, white Americans rebounded from whatever guilt and responsibility they may have felt for allowing the institution of slavery to thrive for more than two hundred years on American soil, and began, once again, to assert their mythic innocence and goodness. They celebrated American democracy while turning away from the hard work of reenvisioning and reconstituting American social and political institutions so that they might become truly democratic; and they believed themselves to be moral and Christian while lynching their African American brothers and sisters who dared to claim the human dignity and rights they deserved. To this audience, so steeped in self-deceit that they could no longer see their actions clearly, Du Bois and Chesnutt sought to unveil not only the depth of their depravity and inhumanity but also the degree to which their subjectivity was being shaped by a refusal to reinvent themselves in the modern era. They demonstrated that the legacy of slavery and the ideology of White supremacy had crippled white Americans and had left an especially deep and festering wound in the collective psyche of white America. In this line of argument, Du Bois and Chesnutt were not far removed from an earlier African American statesman and spokesperson, Frederick Douglass. It was Douglass who, more than four decades earlier in his powerful speech "The Meaning of July Fourth for the Negro," had pointed to the distance White America had drifted from its stated values, charging, "There is not a nation on the earth guilty of practices more shocking and bloody than are the people of the United States, at this very hour" (*Life and Writings*, 2:192). It was Douglass who thundered to listeners, "Americans! Your republican politics, not less than your republican religion, are flagrantly inconsistent. . . . The existence of slavery in this country brands your republicanism as a sham, your humanity as a base pretense, and your Christianity as a lie," revealing the extent of their hypocrisy in celebrating Independence Day while blithely and actively supporting the enslavement of human beings in the "land of the free" (*Life and Writings*, 2:199–200). And it was Douglass who wondered how White Americans resolved in themselves what he believed to be an irreconcilable moral conflict. The later writers perhaps were facing an even greater difficulty than Douglass in unsettling and shifting the perspective of the audience of their day because slavery had been abolished, allowing whites to feel they had completed the necessary work of transforming American society and the White self. Both Du Bois and Chesnutt dramatize in their work, however, the need for white moderates who could recognize and resist the discourses that naturalized white supremacy. Only then, they seem to intuit, could Americans of all shades work to prepare the nation for the modern age.

In 1963, a young Baptist minister by the name of Martin Luther King Jr. was arrested in the city of Birmingham, Alabama, for violating an antidemonstration order. Within days, a letter composed by eight White clergymen in Birmingham was published in a local newspaper calling for patience on the part of African Americans and a calm negotiation between white and black civic leaders in the city. John H. Patton asserts in his article "A Transforming Response: Martin Luther King Jr.'s 'Letter from Birmingham Jail'" that "the public position of these clergy represented the pathway of reasonableness, deliberation, and progress on civil rights to many White and some Black business leaders in Birmingham" (53). For this reason, Patton continues, their letter created a "'rhetorical exigence,' a set of conditions combined with related interests that create an urgent need for response by discourse and argument" (55). The rhetorical exigence in this case was the moral authority that the eight clergymen possessed, the fact that they had positioned themselves not in opposition to desegregation but as supporters of that very goal. Their assertion that King was an unwelcome extremist, especially given their professed support for African American civil rights, had the potential to completely derail the national Civil Rights movement by undermining King's leadership and political strategies. They represented another path to racial equality, one that seemed viable and less contentious, if not as speedy.

By then a well-recognized Civil Rights leader, King spent his week of imprisonment in Birmingham jail composing a response to these clergymen, an open letter that would explain his reasons for coming to Birmingham to lead a campaign against segregation in that city. Troubled by a characterization of his work and his presence as "outside agitation," King articulated a rationale that firmly established him as an insider, both in terms of his organizational ties in Birmingham and his citizenship in the United States. He wrote, now famously, "Injustice anywhere is a threat to justice everywhere. We are caught in an inescapable network of mutuality, tied in a single garment of destiny. Whatever affects one directly, affects all indirectly" (King, "Birmingham Jail," 87). It was in this spirit of interconnectedness that King proceeded to articulate a loving criticism of White America, most specifically the White moderate:

> I must confess that over the past few years I have been gravely disappointed with the white moderate. I have almost reached the regrettable conclusion that the Negro's greatest stumbling block in his stride toward freedom is . . . the white moderate, who is more devoted to "order" than to justice; who prefers a negative peace which is the absence of tension to a positive peace with is the presence of justice; who constantly says "I agree with you in the goal you seek, but I cannot agree with your methods of direct action"; who paternalistically believes he can set the timetable for another man's freedom. . . . Shallow understanding from people of good will is more frustrating than absolute misunderstanding from people of ill will. Lukewarm acceptance is much more bewildering than outright rejection. (96–97)

For King, challenging the passivity, reticence, and flawed reasoning of the White moderate was the key to dislodging America's moral apathy and invigorating the social and moral conscience of the nation.

King does not concern himself with understanding the whys or hows of the White moderate. For him, they are simply an unfortunate reality, a "stumbling block" where he had anticipated allies. The questions of how and why this subject position develops within Whiteness, however, are not inconsequential. How did the average white American come to believe that racial equality could be achieved through any means other than a social and political revolution even as White terroristic violence designed to intimidate and discourage the pursuit of social justice escalated and became more widespread? Why did moderate white Americans believe that racism would end of its own accord even as legal maneuverings to assert and preserve the second-class citizenship of African Americans were well underway? What led white moderates to see themselves as progressive friends rather than the impediments to racial progress that King concluded they were? While these are all important questions with significant implications for Du Bois and Chesnutt, the question was perhaps less about the white moderate than about white *moderation*.

The danger that Du Bois and Chesnutt anticipated, which was given voice by Martin Luther King Jr. sixty years later, was that White double consciousness would retard the development of white antiracist identity and stall efforts at democratic social reform. By intervening in the medical discourse of neurasthenia, Du Bois and Chesnutt offered counternarratives to the myths of Whiteness and sought to "unveil" Whiteness to itself by challenging and undermining supremacist ideologies that were being touted as white mental health. Both writers argued that White double consciousness was a social and psychological ailment that seriously imperiled a young, democratic nation. Du Bois understood White double consciousness as a multifaceted constellation of responses to the reality and presence of multicultural America. Rooted in fears of encountering the subjectivity and gaze of the "Other," White double consciousness was a debilitation that prevented Whiteness from recognizing and dealing with its own moral lapses and timidity, leading to persistent dissimulation and alienation from self and others. It was enabled by the discourses of difference and separation that Whiteness erected all around itself—in its scientific and medical communities, in its legal and political institutions, and in its philosophies and religions. Narratives of regional reconciliation and harmony contributed even further to Whiteness's disconnection from reality because they focused on relationships between white folks, eliding the considerable work needed to create and repair relationships across the color line. In this sociological psychodrama, ultimately the only place where full human connection and mutual recognition was possible, even if only imagined, was in the white psyche. Thus, Du Bois shows, the white moderate was largely an unrealized potential, as the "energy" it would take to break out of this self-reinforcing cycle was largely unavailable to white Americans of any persuasion.

In Chesnutt's creative hands, however, the social and political ramifications of White double consciousness become clear. It is not just that this schizophrenic subjectivity leads to a personal wasting of energies and moral apathy among white people. The more significant problem is that it leads Whiteness *to moderate* its attempts at social justice and reform, inducing whites to deny their individual and collective responsibility for the social ills of the past and present on the one hand, and to approach genuine progressivism only timidly and hesitantly on the other. This moderation, this retreat from the activism that was required to ensure that the United States would pursue genuinely democratic goals, was the danger that both Du Bois and Chesnutt feared. Chesnutt saw that the white moderate could shift from being a person who supports social justice and racial equality to one who, in his or her embrace of white moderation, impedes those very goals. Moreover and more troubling, the commitment to moderation could eventually emerge as a *desirable* subject position for centrist, and often even progressive, white people. Thus, Chesnutt's and Du Bois's engagement with White double consciousness, or what might more usefully be termed "White schizophrenic subjectivity," has significant implications for contemporary America.

Chapter Two

"SHAPING HERSELF INTO A DUTIFUL WIFE"

Demythologizing White Femininity and the
White Home in Frank Yerby's *The Foxes of Harrow*
and Zora Neale Hurston's *Seraph on the Suwanee*

The novel's complexities . . . arise . . . because of her struggle to address
an almost completely buried subject: the interdependent working of
power, race, and sexuality in a white woman's battle for coherence.
—Toni Morrison, "Black Matters," *Playing in the Dark*

People of color have always theorized—but in forms quite
different from the Western form of abstract logic. . . . Our
theorizing . . . is often in narrative forms, in the stories we create.
—Barbara Christian, "The Race for Theory"

The socially constructed image of innocent white womanhood
relies on the continued production of the racist/sexist sexual
myth that black women are not innocent and never can be.
—bell hooks, "Madonna"

White woman. The phrase conjures up images of refinement, elegance, class, and beauty. White women are smart, but not overbearingly so; they are appropriately supportive of their husbands and protective of their beautiful families; they are good mothers. They are gorgeously pale and thin but not enough to suggest illness. They are desirable and desired. They are monied. The White woman is often sheltered and always protected. She is good, kind, and never malicious. She follows her heart and tries to do what is right. When she is wrong, it is because she is misled. White women are luminous. Their Greco-Roman profiles have been sketched, painted, embossed, and projected. Their families and their homes have been explored with gentle interest, as a reflection of their character and worth. They have been idealized, mythologized, and pedestalized. They have been loved.

It would not be until the 1940s that a sustained engagement with the discourse of white femininity and womanhood would emerge within the literature of white estrangement. In that decade alone, however, five novels by African American authors were written or published that specifically interrogated or challenged dominant cultural mythologies about white women's lives and identities. Two of them, Ann Petry's *Country Place* and Zora Neale Hurston's *Seraph on the Suwanee*, are white life novels with storylines centered around female protagonists. Frank Yerby's *The Foxes of Harrow*, also a white life novel, engages the complexity and diversity of white women's psychology and sociology, but the examination is secondary to the central story of the male protagonist. Two other novels that take up the issue of white womanhood and femininity published during this period are not actually white life novels, but, as I argue of one of them in my article "Lillian B. Horace and the Literature of White Estrangement: Rediscovering an African American Intellectual of the Jim Crow Era," these texts have "such a sustained interrogation of Whiteness that I believe it can help us to understand something about how engaged African American intellectuals of the period understood the obstacles facing both White and Black America, particularly women, in twentieth-century Jim Crow America" (Watson, 7). The most famous sketches of white womanhood in this category are Mary Dalton and her mother, Mrs. Dalton, given life in Richard Wright's *Native Son*. In these women (as well as in the patriarch of the family), Wright explores the blindnesses and contradictions of white moderates who claim to desire the social elevation of Black Americans, but whose unexamined White privilege compromises many of their efforts and intentions.[1] The final text I include here is *Angie Brown*, by the recently rediscovered author Lillian B. Horace. In that fiction, the African American title character is the reader's guide to interrogating "the ways of White folks," to borrow Langston Hughes's apt phrasing, with special consideration to the conditions under which a progressive white womanhood can be created and sustained. This chapter focuses on just two of these novels—*The Foxes of Harrow* and *Seraph on the Suwanee*—but such a high level of production on the topic of white womanhood in a single decade, especially given that there had been so little attention directed at white women in the literature of white estrangement during the preceding century, is a clear indication that African American authors thought it important to participate in the cultural conversation about white women that was raging during the 1940s.

African American authors began to engage dominant representations of white womanhood as early as the nineteenth century, but their portrayals during this early period tended to leave the culturally placed halo of white femininity intact. These authors largely represented white womanhood as exalted, for the most part excusing this group of Americans from responsibility for racial and social oppression. For instance, Frederick Douglass described his mistress, Sophia Auld, as a "kind and tender-hearted woman," and was careful to point out that before she was "instructed" by her husband on the proper treatment of slaves, "in the simplicity of her soul she commenced . . . to treat me as she supposed one human being ought to treat another," that is with human recognition, compassion, and kindness. Even after Mrs. Auld ceased to teach Douglass and began, rather, to be yet another White nemesis, he is careful to document and honor who she was before the taint of slavery infected her soul. In writing "she did not adopt this course of treatment [preventing him from being taught to read] immediately," Douglass reminds readers of her innate goodness even as he reveals her moral and spiritual demise (*Narrative*, 66). Self-emancipated author Harriet Jacobs likewise spoke highly of her first mistress, who cared for her so completely that Jacobs recalled of her early years in slavery that her heart was "as free from care as that of any free-born white child" (11). Like Douglass's narrative, Jacobs's *Incidents in the Life of a Slave Girl* emphasizes the Christian piety and humanity of her mistress, not the fact that this woman tacitly supported the system of slavery through her "benevolent" and restrained exercise of power over the enslaved. Jacobs's mistress is saved from the corrupting influence of slavery by an early death, thereby remaining a loving memory for Jacobs, a sanctuary in the narrative as well as within the inhumane institution of slavery.

In these memories and sketches of white women, Douglass and Jacobs help to establish a pattern for representing white womanhood that will continue throughout the early twentieth century: they uphold the myth of a kind, sympathetic, and moral white woman. The white mistress is portrayed as a site and source of comfort within the plantation culture. She provides human recognition of and compassion for the suffering of others, teaches the illiterate and counsels the unredeemed, and bravely loves across the color line as part of her Christian responsibility. White women participating in the system of slavery may not exercise their influence beyond the metaphorical hearth, but in ruling with the heart, they domesticate the institution, making the system one in which human connection can be imagined as possible.

But a further analysis is also suggested by the two sketches of exalted White femininity found in these classic narratives of slavery. Both highlight the *potential* embodied in the myths surrounding white womanhood and lament the failures of white women to live up to that ideal. During the nineteenth century, diverse publications aimed at a female audience—from women's magazines to literature to how-to manuals—instructed women that their power resided in their subordinated positions, that the proper performance of femininity was essential for the successful functioning not only of the individual home but also of the youthful nation. Being protected from the influences of capitalism and the strain of political engagement, women, the argument went, were free from the very interactions and responsibilities that might corrupt their moral sensibilities. They were to be the bastions of purity and piety, able through their Christian-centered lives to reorient and recenter men (fathers, brothers, husbands, and sons), whose moral compasses had been set adrift by engagement with an immoral world. This cultural discourse surrounding the role of women, especially as articulated through the Cult of True Womanhood,[2] suggested a sort of nineteenth-century White *Woman's* Burden, a certain responsibility for them to speak up about, and even to resist, the wrongs of their societies. In the North, the image of the idealized white woman was used to galvanize white female political action both in and outside of the home. This implicit call to action spawned the emergence of women's sewing societies and other efforts to support those escaping slavery, women's direct involvement in the abolitionist and temperance movements, and a lively period of women's literary production. Thus one senses in the sketches of Jacobs and Douglass an unarticulated longing, a desire that white women—whose unsullied Christian foundation should set them apart and give them power to effect change—should *do* something with the power invested in them as moral guardians of the family, and by extension, the nation. But the critique is subtle, and is really only suggested by the presence of women who *do* help Douglass and Jacobs in their bids for freedom and autonomy.

Women like Mrs. Auld and Jacobs's mistress—women who are innately "good" but corrupted by the system of slavery—are not the only representations of white femininity included in Douglass's and Jacobs's autobiographies. Both texts also include sketches of debased white womanhood—women who are mean-spirited, jealous, and violent. Juxtaposed to the white mistresses striving to maintain their Christian training in the demoralizing system of slavery, these are women who actively abandon their feminine sensibilities to participate in racist violence. Douglass invokes them when he includes the story of Mrs. Giles Hick, who beat one of her servants to death with her own hands because she found the enslaved woman "slow to move," or when he describes the humiliated plantation mistress who "is never better pleased than when she sees them [her husband's mulatto children] under the lash" (*Narrative*, 58, 43). Jacobs includes this class of women in her sketches of Mrs. Wade, who "lashed the slaves with the might of a man," and Mrs. Flint, her jealous mistress, who behaves erratically enough to cause Jacobs to fear for her life (41). But even in most of these moments, white women appear more the victims of, rather than collaborators with, the racism of their societies. They are made sympathetic even in their ferocity, a rhetorical approach that preserves the myth of white women as essentially good.

But this second group of images does more than simply expose the failures—however gently—of specific white women. These portraits of women who actively support racism and slavery anticipate a period when the definitions of the idealized white woman will change. By the dawn of the twentieth century, silence, obedience, and loyalty to the institutions of the South will be celebrated in women as the qualities that define a "lady." No longer will it be implied that women should seek to intervene, through their influence over men or through any other means, in the social and political apparatuses of America. Rather, a new cultural icon of white femininity will emerge, that of the Southern belle. Made popular in Lost Cause and Southern Agrarian fiction and early Hollywood plantation films, the figure of the finely dressed and lovingly indulged Southern belle presented the white woman as little more than an attractive coquette, a morally passive, decorative object "doing nothing, nothing" as a condition of her social acceptance (Dyer, 187). As she was sketched, the belle was scarcely religious, had no interest in politics, and did not trouble herself with questions of morality. She was more interested in manipulating her own image than seeking to improve her society's social wrongs. Made more beautiful by an implicit comparison to Black women who were represented as unattractive and unfeminine in most popular media, and made more "lady-like" by the presence of black servants who relieved her of all need for labor whether in the home or outside, the belle marked white women as frivolous and superficial adornment like never before in the discourse of femininity. And, as Tara McPherson persuasively argues in *Reconstructing Dixie*, the "hyperfeminized figure of the southern woman" traveled far beyond the South and performed cultural work throughout the nation (19).

The belle worked on many levels, all of which led the nation to reimagine the South as a pastoral Eden in which the challenges of race and class had been effectively managed and resolved. She became a "discursive symbol for the region" who softened, if not completely erased, the realities of a violently oppressive racial caste system and an abusive class system that benefited few Southerners—black or white—in the nineteenth century (McPherson, 19). In fact, the sexual vulnerability of the belle, which became such a focus of postbellum media and popular culture, did much to suggest that the strict race and class hierarchies of the South were needed throughout the nation as social organizing principles. Having earned the loyalty of her enslaved Black servants and the respect and admiration of lower-class white Southerners, the belle also held out the promise that a harmonious society could flourish despite severe social, political, and economic inequity, a suggestion that white Americans throughout the war-torn nation were desperate to hear. Additionally, the belle's dependency and political inexperience provided justification for the role of the white patriarch at a time when white Southern men were trying to reestablish themselves in the aftermath of the political and economic defeats of the Civil War; it effectively allowed the group to retain their investment in the race and class distinctions that defined the antebellum South rather than engage in the work of reconceptualizing themselves as Southerners and as Americans. And the figure also suggested to other women that "proper femininity" would be rewarded with social and economic elevation and cultural reverence. Thus, the belle facilitated regional reconciliation largely by presenting the Civil War as a national disgrace that deposed genteel white ladies from their proper pedestals and that overturned the proper order by empowering black men.

As I've said, the popularity and widespread appeal of the belle marked a dramatic shift in the cultural discourse and mythology of the ideal white woman. The value of this white woman, indeed her very femininity, resided in her unquestioning support of the patriarchal order and her commitment to White supremacy and class elitism as the hallmarks of White (Southern) life. Unanchored from her particular region, this image of idealized

White femininity did much to circumscribe the ways that all women of the period could imagine and construct themselves while remaining within the parameters of acceptable femininity, and did much to mythologize white female *disengagement* as the norm and ideal of White femininity. It was an ideal that gained additional weight by the religious and scientific sexism of the nineteenth century. In *The Remembered Gate: Origins of American Feminism*, Barbara J. Berg documents the variety of cultural discourses that espoused "the doctrines of feminine weakness, inferiority, and submission," reinforcing widely held beliefs that women were too emotional and naïve to understand the complexities of American life. Biblical teachings often held that women's most important duties were to be discreet, obedient, and concerned only with the smooth functioning of the home; science suggested that women possessed an emotional temperament that was biologically grounded, making them irrational and unfit for intellectual engagement. Artists painted and sculpted women as pure and evangelical (and White), or, in the alternative, as debased and corrupt (and darkened). These theorems were then indoctrinated in both sexes from their earliest formal and informal educational experiences (Berg, 76–84). This image of the physically and intellectually weak woman was cultivated at practically all levels of nineteenth-century culture, becoming a seemingly monolithic cultural articulation of women's identity. It not only formed the basis for understanding womanhood but also provided the parameters within which women shaped their particular performances of femininity. Much like what has been argued of African Americans in this country, their understandings and articulations of themselves as women were always in rhetorical dialogue with these master narratives.

By the late 1930s, yet another cultural conversation about White femininity began to emerge. It seemed both timely and necessary, as many of the fundamental gender (and racial) norms that had structured white women's lives had dramatically shifted after the turn of the century. Foremost among these changes was the fact that many middle-class white women had entered the workforce and joined the military during the First and later the Second World War. When they may have been resistant to entering the workforce, white women were told through government propaganda like the 1942–1943 "Get a War Job" campaign that employment outside the home was part of their patriotic duty and that their labor was necessary if the nation was to be victorious (Walsh, 52). The absence of men due to the wars also meant that a significant number of women had full responsibility for sustaining their homes and families, enabling them, as a group, to experience a different level of autonomy and accomplishment in work and family. Mass media responded to this new reality with a dynamic set of representations of women during this period. Newspapers and magazines routinely ran articles like the ones published in *Ladies' Home Journal* that showcased women pilots and machinists (Hymowitz and Weissman, 312); the well-known advertisement featuring Rosie the Riveter was joined by military photographs of female WAVES, SPARs, and WACs,[3] and sexually provocative images of women adorned fighter planes (May, 62). Hollywood sensationalized the image of the modern working woman even further by releasing a number of films during the late 1930s and 1940s that featured successful working women for whom romance and/or marriage were not the only priorities. Part of the glamour of a fictional Laura, Gilda, or Scarlett[4] was the fact that they relied on their own intelligence to overcome the personal and societal challenges that threatened to overwhelm them. The cultural interest in the accomplished modern woman even led to the expansion of the film industry's advertising machine, the "star system," to more fully include (and capitalize on) the popularity of actresses during this period.

But the tectonic shifts that interwar and postwar America faced went beyond just the roles of women. In the 1940s, under the banner of preserving democracy, the United States entered a world war, witnessed the atrocities and depravity of the Holocaust, and dropped atomic bombs on two Japanese cities, killing approximately 250,000 people, mostly civilians. The Cold War followed on the heels of armed conflict, and the fear of communist infiltration of American political and economic structures was rampant. African Americans began more vocal agitation for social and political rights in America through the Double V campaign,[5] the lobbying and legal efforts of the NAACP, and other civil rights initiatives, while White Southerners, in particular, intensified their opposition to full citizenship for black Americans. Race riots erupted in U.S. cities throughout the country. Thus, the forties was another decade, like the 1930s before or 1960s afterward, in which white Americans felt the tremendous uncertainty of a nation moving forward and recognized that the America that emerged after this watershed period could be quite different indeed from that which had preceded it. For most White Americans, the thought was terrifying.

But for White women, perhaps, the possibilities were as exhilarating as they were terrifying. After generations of being taught that their "proper" place was in the home and having that dictate reinforced by restrictive laws and social expectations, middle- and upper-class White women were finally given sanction to enter the labor force. Once there, they found the ability to earn their own money and to make decisions about the use of that income to support their families and themselves appealing. But these new laborers were attracted by more than the hope of financial security; many of them also found personal fulfillment from their employment outside the home (Chafe, 179). So when male veterans returned home to reclaim the positions held by female wartime workers, women were not enthusiastic about losing their jobs. According to Carol Hymowitz and Michaele Weissman, "At the beginning of the war, 95 percent of women workers intended to quit when their men came home. By war's end they had changed their minds. More than 80 percent wanted to continue working" (313–314). The reluctance to return to prewar norms of domesticity was palpable enough that new government and popular messaging campaigns were launched urging women to "step down" and "step aside" for returning vets. When ultimately forced out of positions, occupations, and industries by the returning male laborers, discriminatory labor practices, and an unsupportive public opinion, women successfully sought alternative employment opportunities. By the early 1950s, more women were in the workforce than during the war (Hymowitz and Weissman, 314).

The necessity of women in the workplace during wartime challenged the very foundation of the American patriarchal family by demonstrating the intelligence and strength of women and their capacity to make sound decisions to advance individual and collective well-being, even in the absence of male leadership or "protection." However, much like the experience of African American veterans who had fought to preserve democracy abroad only to be told upon their return that they should accept their second-class citizenship as "natural," middle- and upper-class women, too, were urged to forget the freedoms they had enjoyed while the nation was at war and to embrace their identities as supportive wives and mothers. Andrea Walsh's important analysis of this period strongly suggests that the debate about women's "reconversion" to traditional gender roles was presented as one of social utility: "Mothering was stressed as central for postwar women, and central not only for children. The returning veteran, with physical and emotional scars, sorely needed attention . . . women would ease America back to normalcy" (75–76). But the cultural demand that white women return to the home and their traditional roles within it evidenced more than a simple argument of convenience or social necessity;

the imperative constituted a battle over the very "nature" of White womanhood. In a time when there was "growing sense that it was now more difficult than ever before to ground one's conduct in a stable system of values," this dictate sought to fix an image of the White family and home that had been destabilized by women as laborers and heads of household (Graebner, 19). Traditional gender roles and family structures emerged as a central symbol of stability and normality. But these roles, particularly those of the unemployed housewife and wage-earning husband who was the sole provider for the family, were the fairly exclusive province of middle- and upper-class Whiteness. This class and race exclusivity passing as the norm effectively positioned a narrow but mythologized Whiteness as the barometer of "respectable morality" for all Americans (Lott, 88). Thus, reestablishing the dominance of the traditional family, and the woman's role within it, helped to secure the dominance of White masculinity and the desirability of Whiteness simultaneously.

While dominant cultural messages were monotonously echoing "return home, white woman," the literature of white exposure that I examine in this chapter instead focuses on the psychological and emotional lives of the women enshrined in those domestic spaces. As white women were being touted as the mechanism through which the nation would heal and find its way back to "traditional American values," Frank Yerby and Zora Neale Hurston foregrounded the costs that white women often pay to conform to this narrow ideal of White femininity. And while popular culture eagerly imagined the white home as a protected space that enabled white women to fulfill a necessary role in domestic, social, and political economies, *Foxes* and *Seraph* reveal the home as contentious and unsafe for white women. In this place, their understandings and desires for themselves come into conflict with the cultural mandates laid out for them. But, ironically, it is also the space that provides the relationships and interpersonal exchanges that enable them to resolve those conflicts and to navigate their performances of femininity in socially acceptable ways. It is this final claim about the white home—that it is both antagonistic to and a supportive foundation for the conflicted psychology of white women—that positions *Foxes* and *Seraph* as important theoretical frameworks for understanding white female subjectivity. These authors dramatize the psychological maneuverings necessary to make race and class elitism desirable to white women who are themselves marginalized. The picture that emerges is one that directly challenges the mythology of white womanhood, tearing down the pedestal and replacing it with images of complex, conflicted women who are as much villain as hero, victim as victimizer.

The Foxes of Harrow was Frank Yerby's first published novel. It was quickly purchased by Twentieth Century-Fox and released in 1947 as a film, making Yerby the first African American author to have a literary work adapted into film by a major Hollywood studio.[6] He built his career writing almost exclusively white life fiction, and consequently his largely white reading audience typically was not aware of his racial background. Yet, or perhaps even because of the path he chose for his work, he was one of the most prolific and popular African American writers of his generation. According to Gene Andrew Jarrett, Yerby published thirty-three novels during his career, with impressive success:

> Three were translated into film, one for television, twelve were bestsellers; almost all were selections of the Book of the Month Club; they have been translated into over thirty languages; and, to date, over sixty million copies of them have been sold around the world. ("Frank Yerby," 197)

Yet because his accomplishments signaled his popularity with a primarily nonacademic readership, Yerby has been largely ignored by the scholarly community. To date there has been no full-length critical study of Yerby's work, and fewer than two dozen articles have been published on his extensive corpus. James L. Hill, who has arguably done the most to gain for Yerby's work a critical audience, writes that Yerby has been marginalized because his popular fiction "pitted him squarely between two literary worlds, one whose overt racial ideology he flatly rejected and the other which generally ignored him because of the genre of fiction he had chosen to write" (144). But, like Hill, I believe that Yerby's work has much to offer readers, especially those interested in the contributions of African American writers to the critical discourse on Whiteness. Yerby, as Darwin T. Turner first articulated in 1968, "has debunked historical myths relentlessly" in his long literary career, making this his "major contribution to American culture" and qualifying him as an American writer worth reading (572).

Yerby's intervention into the cultural discourse on Whiteness is at once bold and subtle. Echoing the insights offered by W. J. Cash in *The*

Mind of the South (1941), Turner highlights the myriad ways that Yerby attacks directly the myths of the American South:

> The South, he [Yerby] has pointed out, was founded by adventurers, out-
> casts, and failures who migrated to America because they had nothing to
> lose; the actual aristocrats, having nothing to gain by emigration, remained
> on the continent. By exploiting people and the land, these immigrants
> amassed fortunes. Accustomed only to indolence and luxury, their children
> and grandchildren created the legends about aristocratic heritage. (573)

Yerby also challenges the very foundations of Whiteness by creating White homes, families, and communities that are anything but ideal. White men kill each other seeking to gain advantage over one another; white women are in competition with each other as well as women of color for the roman-tic attention of powerful white men; white progeny are narcissistic, cruel, and petty; and communities are formed and destroyed by the ruthless and selfish ambitions of the few. In Yerby's White worlds there is opportunity, but only for those who are willing to eschew social laws and mores in favor of a "looser" moral compass. Those who succeed are always calculating and opportunistic, often thieves, adulterers, and murderers. And while Yerby himself identified the "very strong defense of Black history and Black people" as a common theme of his work, one cannot overlook the consistency with which he also seeks to estrange racial Whiteness, mak-ing it possible for us to see "the workings of . . . [its] entrails" more clearly (Maryemma Graham, 70; Du Bois, "White Folk," 923).

In the midst of these largely masculine dystopias, Yerby also often creates complex, self-aware white women, making his commentary about Whiteness broader than that which is offered by much white life fiction. In engaging the construction of White femininity, for instance, Yerby seems interested in how gendered and racial discourses of a par-ticular period affected women's understandings of themselves. Are white women of the South less likely to be oppressors or do they typically sup-port the hierarchical, racist structures of their societies? Do they look to disrupt a range of social strictures in seeking a measure of autonomy or do they simply accept the protections afforded them by the racial and gender conventions of their societies? While there is certainly a range of representations of White femininity presented in Yerby's work, he seems to have a particular interest in the figure of the white lady, the belle, as a character though whom these questions of gendered, racial identity can be considered. Thus, attentively engaging the psychology and sociology of Yerby's belles becomes a key opportunity to think about the broader implications of gender and class to cultural discourses about Whiteness in the 1940s.

As I have already noted, the image and representation of the Southern belle was well established by the turn of the twentieth century. As a symbol, the belle had been used to represent the gentility and beauty of antebellum Southern culture, to insinuate that familial bonds and mutual connection commonly existed between White slaveholders and their Black slaves, and to suggest the grace and dignity of a deposed Southern aristocracy. She had been brought to iconic life in films such as *The Birth of a Nation*, *Jezebel*, and most famously *Gone with the Wind*, where her determination and resilience served to make her a heroic figure rather than a nefarious supporter of racial inequality. But by the time that Yerby was writing *Foxes*, due largely to shifting cultural norms and the pressure of the NAACP on Hollywood studios for more evenhanded treatment of African Americans in film, images of the misunderstood and wrongly defeated South (and her belles) had waned. New images of White femininity were emerging, especially in film noir, that painted White women as professional, sexually self-possessed, and modern, albeit with a dark underside of intrigue and danger about them. The settings of many films of the era were urban and industrial, not the rural South, and white actresses were often filmed in ways that accentuated their Whiteness without the obvious contrast of Black bodies. In fact, in film noir, corporeal Blackness was almost completely erased by the use of exclusively white casts and story lines, thus holding out the promise of a world in which blackness has been contained, if not completely neutralized. The threat of evil and moral degeneracy was represented not by the presence of actual blacks, but by abject white bodies that became figuratively (and sometimes literally) darker as their fall from Whiteness became more pronounced. White women were the promise of these celluloid worlds, because they could be cleansed of their improper desires and returned to the social function of reproducing the proper White home and family. But in returning to the antebellum South and the myth of the belle in *The Foxes of Harrow*, Yerby seems to be challenging a discourse that would once again refuse to see the centrality of Blackness to White racial identity. His presentation of the belle Odalie Arceneaux foregrounds that Whiteness generally, and White femininity specifically, is a hybridized identity, one that is always already in a rhetorical dialogue with Blackness.

71

Tara McPherson's work is again useful here. In *Reconstructing Dixie*, she describes an evolution of racial imaginaries that has changed the ways in which "Black" and "White" are understood as being in relation to one another. She writes that "early-twentieth-century racial logics tended to delineate Whiteness in sharp contrast to Blackness, [but] by mid-century other modes of framing Whiteness were developing, modes that tended to repress the relations between White and Black." Coining the term "lenticular logic of racial visibility" to explain why the complexity and diversity of racial relations in this country are not more fully captured in our cultural products, she argues that lenticular logic is a:

> monocular logic, a schema by which histories or images that are actually copresent get presented (structurally, ideologically) so that only one of the images can be seen at a time. Such an arrangement represses connection, allowing Whiteness to float free from Blackness, denying the long historical imbrications of racial markers and racial meanings in the South. (7)

The belle, she persuasively demonstrates, has been used in just such a manner. However, Yerby's representation of the Southern lady disrupts this lenticular logic by forcing readers to confront the impossibility of racial separation in U.S. society or psychology, making him less a historical debunker than a radical reenvisioner of Southern White culture. This reenvisioning begins not with the mythical locus of White purity—the body of the White woman—but with her miscegenated mind.

Set in Louisiana between the years 1825 and 1865, *The Foxes of Harrow* offers an extended examination of the culture and politics of antebellum Creole society and its connection to White American identity. The novel is an epic story that traces the life of Stephen Fox, an Irish gambler and newcomer to America. Stephen is a determined, savvy, calculating man who not only amasses wealth, a stately plantation, and the high regard of an antebellum Southern Creole community but also becomes quintessentially American during his journey to social standing and financial success. Beginning the novel as a rogue with one asset to his name, a pristinely white pearl that he will eventually use to finance his acquisition of land, slaves, and equipment, Stephen exhibits an unwavering determination to achieve his ultimate desire, the beautiful and elusive Creole heiress, Odalie Arceneaux. He is immediately smitten by her loveliness but is also drawn to the challenge that she presents, for no man has been able to win Odalie's heart or hand. When Stephen does so, it is a conquest that provides the final piece of his social legitimacy and establishes him as a powerful patriarch and leader within the community. His social birth secured by marriage into a respected Creole family, he seeks to establish a dynasty: "The Foxes were here in this new world to stay. And not merely to stay—to lead it, rule it, leave their mark upon it. Having no ancestors, he told himself, I am become one" (139).

Stephen's ascension, however, is not primarily the result of his individual effort. Yerby carefully demonstrates that Stephen's social mastery, and even his American-ness and his Whiteness, are mediated through the presence, talent, labor, and folk wisdom of enslaved Black people. For instance, his first lesson on what it means to be a White American occurs very early in the novel, during a conversation with Mike Farrel, the captain who rescues him when he has been ejected from a steamboat for the ungentlemanly act of cheating at cards. To pass the time as they head for New Orleans, Farrel tells stories about life on the river and points out the place where slave mutineers were hanged, referring to those who were murdered as "Nigras." But when Stephen prompts Mike for more information, he (Stephen) asks about the "*blacks*" who were hung (8). He has yet to learn and adopt the racial lexicon that will reflect his Whiteness. In responding, though, Farrel's language never allows the victims even the smallest modicum of respect or humanity, and the next time Stephen refers to a black person, he, too, uses the term "Nigra," proving Toni Morrison's insight that the path to becoming American is typically through the adoption of anti-Black rhetoric and sentiment (Yerby, *Foxes*, 26).[7] Yerby's text bears this out even further when Stephen meets and befriends a young Creole aristocrat named Andre Le Blanc. When Andre attempts to explain why some of the apparently "white" women were dressed like slaves, Stephen replies, "I don't see how ye Frenchmen do it, Andre. To me there is nothing on earth so repulsive as a black. To sleep with that old monkey—ugh!" (27). Here, his professed aversion distinguishes him as "American" as well as White. Stephen's transformation from Irishman to White American is effected in the narrative through his use of the appropriate racialized language and exhibition of the proper attitudes toward blacks.

Once those basic lessons are learned, it is but a short step to buying in to the unreflective, unquestioned consumption and exploitation of the enslaved. Stephen's financial success, social standing, and indeed his very life are made possible by the labor, knowledge, and expertise of those he now claims to own. When he is shot in a duel and believed close to death, one of his slaves rumored to be a voodoo priestess, Tante Caleen, tends to his wound. She is responsible for a brief marital reunion between Stephen and his wife as well as for saving the life of their son, Etienne, after he falls ill with yellow fever. When other planters lose everything to a storm, Stephen harvests early and makes a significant profit because Caleen has forewarned him about the storm. She is, as Phyllis Klotman highlights in "A Harrowing Experience: Frank Yerby's First Novel to Film," a character "whose importance in the novel cannot be overestimated" (220). Equally important, however, is the fact that Stephen is also dependent on the enslaved who clear the land, plant and harvest the crops, and erect the rudimentary housing that provides shelter until he can afford more. Yerby demonstrates that what is typically thought of as White intelligence and effort is really dependency masquerading as mastery. As an unpropertied gambler, Stephen literally has no knowledge or experience that will ensure his success as a planter. He relies completely on skin-color privilege and the coercive power of Whiteness to make his fortune and his mark.

Interestingly, Yerby foreshadows early on the degree to which Stephen will cherish, protect, and trade on his Whiteness to gain success. The pearl that is his sole possession is described as pristine white: "Now it was milky, now like snow; now it was seafoam breaking white . . . now it was moonmist" (32). Stephen admits that, although he does not understand why he has sacrificed so much to hold onto the pearl, he has "fought like all the devils in hell to keep it. I've never owned it . . . always it owned me" (51). The pearl became a promise of what his life could be, a symbol of wealth, status, and ease. He does not know how he will earn the right to wear the pearl until he goes to the South and sees what Whiteness can buy him: the ability to live "graciously, with leisure to cultivate the tastes and to indulge every pleasure" (23). It is in antebellum New Orleans that he understands Whiteness as the path to an aristocratic existence marked by "mastery over this earth" and the ability to "stride this American soil unafraid, never needing to cheat and lie and steal" (24). Yet innocence is not available to Stephen if he is to pursue his dream; the class and race hierarchies of the antebellum South all but *ensure* that he will have to "cheat and lie and steal" to establish himself. But the dream (or, perhaps, fantasy) of that kind of freedom—the ability to remake himself into something valuable and valued—possesses Stephen even before he has the words to articulate his desire. By trading carefully on racial Whiteness as both identity and ideology, he can fully embody the promise of the immaculate pearl.

Odalie, the quintessential Southern belle and the woman Stephen decides will be the mistress of his plantation, Harrow, is equally reliant upon the enslaved, but in ways that are different from those exhibited by her husband-to-be. Where Stephen exploits Blackness in very direct and active ways, Odalie relies on an Africanist presence to understand herself as a privileged and free White woman. She is invested in the cultural scripts about Black women in particular: that they are sexually unrestrained, and in antebellum New Orleans, literally prostitutes; that they are overly exuberant and emotionally intemperate; and that they have no preference in suitor or mate. These are all myths that served the institution of slavery broadly but that also worked to preserve distinctions between the legally recognized institution of white marriage and the commonplace and highly formalized practice of plaçage[8] in antebellum New Orleans. It is a vision of black womanhood that she has internalized and against which she positions herself largely because Odalie has begun to sense, if only dimly, the parallels between her position as a kept White lady and that of the enslaved, commodified Black woman.

Odalie articulates her understanding of the tenuous position that belles occupy within her culture during an exchange she has with Stephen early in their courtship. Their light repartee foreshadows the shift that is about to occur in the relationship, as Odalie begins to reveal her affections—and fears—to him. In this exchange, though, Stephen seems almost distracted; he watches the movement of "the wine-red lips" as she speaks and thinks to himself that all of his effort to establish himself has been "insignificant against the gaining of this woman." At this moment Odalie says, "It pleases me to know that I meant more to you than—than a horse. . . . You seemed a bold devil—utterly careless and reckless of anything or anyone that you wanted. I was unaccustomed to being looked at appraisingly like a slave girl" (115). Her statement, delivered at the precise moment when Stephen is sizing her up like an object he is about to purchase, is a clear indication that Odalie's read of her culture and her position within it is on the mark: she is, like the people of color all around her, more object than subject. At moments like these—as common as the exchanges between male and female relatives or heterosexual couples can be—the fact of her tenuous hold on a socially recognized and valued subjectivity threatens to explode into her consciousness. The only hedge against the intrusion of this knowledge into the white woman's consciousness is the mask that society wears to cloak the imbalances of power and recognition that are systemically bred between white women and men. Clearly one of those masks is "race." In the moment she chooses to chastise Stephen for his failure to regard her differently than he would "a slave girl," she not only points out his breach of propriety but also deploys race as a means of negotiating power in the relationship. She takes Stephen to task for being "careless" and "reckless"—one might say, ungentlemanly—in failing to act as if the social distinctions between Southern belles and enslaved women have weight, force, and meaning. Odalie seeks to reassert a structural and social distance from black women who are her point of internal comparison, and in the process uses race (and, to a lesser extent, class) to reclaim the privilege and protections afforded the status of lady in her culture.

What also becomes clear in this first extended conversation between Odalie and Stephen is how profoundly her performance of White upper-class femininity has been structured around her perceptions of, and desires for, clear, unbreachable distinctions between black and white women. Believing, as she has been led, that Black women are sexually indiscriminate, she adopts a performance of White femininity that not only fulfills but also exceeds her society's expectations for female purity and respectability. For her, being a White lady is about withholding herself and withdrawing from others because those are the very choices that she perceives are unavailable to Black women. She is aloof to the point of frigidity, a performance intended to bring the distance between her and other raced (and classed) women of the community into sharper relief. Her investment in a racial lenticular logic forces her to assert a distinction between herself and black women where there is actually very little difference. In so doing, however, Odalie becomes more deeply invested in the race and class hierarchies that exist in the antebellum South—calling upon Stephen to recognize her superior value precisely because she is an upper-class White woman—as a means of structuring her identity.

It does not occur to Odalie, of course, that her expression of upper-class White femininity could be anything other than celebrated and desired. She has been indulged by family and community, her beauty a source of strength, her rejection of male attention only serving to heighten her desirability. Having adopted this hyperfeminine performance of untouchable beauty, she believes that she has finally fixed the distinction between herself and Black women of lower classes. But when she discovers that her husband has taken a "quadroon" lover, the facade of her power falls away. She spits at him, "You've come home to me night after night with your lips still warm from the kisses of your Negress! . . . What under heaven could possess you to ride fifteen miles to visit a mulatto wench? . . . I must know what this thing is—I must know!" (215). When she threatens to have his lover whipped, Stephen insinuates that he will leave her. His retort provides a clear indication of the embattled and conflicting definitions of "wife" at work in their home and society: "She has been a better companion to me than ever ye could dream of. She is twice the woman, and thrice the wife that ever ye were. Remember this, my dear—no man ever leaves a *good* wife" (215). In this moment, perhaps for the first time, Odalie senses that Stephen has wanted something more of her than her grudging submission. She seems truly lost; despite her physical and emotional inaccessibility, it is unfathomable to her that Stephen could prefer a Black woman to her. She is stunned to find that, after all, there is little difference between her and any other woman that Stephen Fox chooses to acquire. There are no cultural mandates that he remain monogamous as there are for her, and because he is responsible for her financial support as well as her social status, she has more at stake should their marriage fail. So while Odalie's internal barometer has assured her that her performance of femininity places her above the black women all around her, her investment in the Whiteness of her femininity has left her utterly unprepared for the reality of competing articulations of feminine identity. It has left her grasping for a connection with others that she, herself, has foreclosed.

While Odalie has clearly limited the expression of her humanity in her narrow and restricted performance of femininity, she is not totally to blame for her inability to connect emotionally and sexually with her husband. Yerby also explores through her character the tenuous foundation of the White family. He locates the instability of this mythic and heralded social institution in the socially ascribed dominance of men as well as the freedom they have to pursue sexual encounters outside of marriage and "race," which gives them no incentive to truly commit—physically or emotionally—to their wives. Odalie articulates this analysis when she describes the sexual advances of men as being "fawned at" and explains, "There's something—well—private here . . . something inviolable. And men are such beasts!" (84). Stereotypically, perhaps, she desires something more than the physical union that seems to be the purpose of marriage during this historical period, but Stephen is completely unable (and has no incentive) to respond to Odalie's emotional needs, only promising that he will be patient and gentle when they consummate their marriage. He assumes that once they are married, securing for her the respectability of that institution, he will have full access to her emotionally as well as physically. In fact, after only a few weeks of waiting for Odalie to set the date of their wedding, he decides he has "worked too long, and waited too long" and that he will not be denied any further. His intentions are ambiguous, but the "advance" that follows is described as an assault:

> He bent his head down and *locked* his lips expertly *against* hers . . . his arms *tightened*, so that she would have *cried out in pain* had she been able. But her mouth was against his, stopping her cries, stopping her breath. She *hammered* at his chest with both hands, but he *drove his iron hand* inward at the small of her back so that her body *ground against* his. (124–125; emphasis mine)

Odalie's domination and concomitant silencing is romanticized in this moment, with Stephen cast as the strong, masterful hero and Odalie as the properly *un*desiring woman, a scenario that recalls Ann duCille's analysis of "romantic fiction's frightening fixation with rape as a prelude to everlasting love" (126). Yet it seems important to note that Stephen approaches physical intimacy with his future wife in much the same way he has pursued her: he single-mindedly hammers away at her until her defenses finally fall and he is free to secure his victory over her. At times his assault is a full frontal barrage; at others he withdraws to lull his opponent into a false sense of security. With either tactic, however, the goal remains the complete domination of his opponent. Once Odalie begins to respond to his aggressive advance, he releases her and demands that they set a date on which they will be married. Her desire for him becomes his ultimate weapon against her, and nowhere in this equation is there space to consider the needs or fears Odalie has articulated. Their union is set as the transaction that will finally allow him full access to her body.

Marriage, however, does not secure access to Odalie's emotional life, nor does it calm her fears of physical intimacy. She is terrified by the idea of consummating their marriage, "trembling so violently that he [Stephen] could see it even across the vast bedroom" and involuntarily responding by fighting against his advances (128). Her cries of terror are met by hard kisses and steely arms drawing her toward him. But just before she is raped, Stephen once again releases her and leaves the room.[9] Her fear and inability to give herself to him is met by an "icy, echoing emptiness" in him (128). The fairy tale union is thwarted. There is no passionate and harmonious White home. Instead, we are offered an uneasy resolution, for when Odalie does force herself to return to her husband on their wedding night, it is only with thoughts of submission and children. Internally she wails,

This—this was marriage! This was how a man expressed the tenderness that was within him and the devotion. Then human beings *were* animals after all and no better than the other animals despite all the lace and perfume and poetry. . . . And there were years of this before her, years of steeling herself to submit, and shaping herself into a dutiful wife. Yet she must. (129)

Odalie clearly understands that her options are limited as an upper-class woman and a wife. For her, becoming a dutiful wife requires opening herself to a sexual act that does not meet her emotional needs for safety or connection. Stephen's dissatisfaction with his life as a married man is channeled into a relationship with a mulatta mistress.

Odalie's discovery that her performance of the hyperfeminized Southern belle may actually cost her her marriage opens her to the assistance of the mystical Tante Caleen. Through Caleen's folk wisdom and the intervention of another powerful voodoo priestess whose assistance Caleen enlists, Odalie finally comes to understand that she has shut down part of herself in an attempt to secure a vision of herself as separate from Blackness. She is lectured by the second priestess, Selada, on what has gone wrong in her marriage: "If Madame could once forget herself, if Madame could for once *want* Monsieur—instead of passively submitting—then Madame would learn that love is the most wonderful gift of God, in which fierceness and tenderness are so entwined that never can they be separated, and abasement linked with exaltation." Odalie finds herself wondering after she has participated in the ritual orchestrated by Selada, "Could a woman be too good?" (221). Thus, the Odalie who emerges from the ritual questions, for the first time, the utility of a racialized femininity that places her on a pedestal, unreachable and cold. This does not free her of the deeply held beliefs about what constitutes an appropriate performance of White femininity, but it does awaken her to the possibility of other ways of thinking of herself as a raced and gendered woman. In a highly suggestive exchange that parallels Scarlett's famous grooming scene in *Gone with the Wind*, Caleen serves as midwife for Odalie's feminine rebirth. However, in *Foxes*, the belle's enslaved attendant does more than simply usher her into the important yet ultimately superficial performances of White femininity—dress, conversation, social protocols, and the like. Here, Caleen is responsible for reshaping Odalie's psychology such that she is able to see herself not only as a lady but also as a carnal, fully embodied female. The distinction is important. As Bridget T. Heneghan explains in *Whitewashing America: Material Culture and Race in the Antebellum Imagination*, "feminine" participated in a set of binaries—feminine and masculine, as well as feminine and female. "Female" designated the corporeal woman, the body made concrete through manual labor or physical marking—blackness, deformity, slovenliness. Sarah Josepha Hale, editor of *Godey's Lady's Book*, descries the use of the term "female" because it insists on the body. . . . "Female" signifies a physical form, and therefore ungenders the feminine. (87–88)

Odalie is brought into a rebirth ritual that brings her in touch with her physicality and the pleasures of the body, the very things that would "ungender" her according to conventional thinking. The presence of these "darker" aspects of her self have been denied, but, as she is to discover, they are present within her and repressed through the feminine performance that she has asserted as her complete self. When Caleen has completed her ritual of awakening—which includes verbal, visual, and tactile stimulation and manipulation of the belle—Odalie smiles at her seminude image in a mirror. She is aware of a "warmth stealing slowly and subtly along the hidden surface of her flesh" and goes in search of her husband (225). Thus awakened and brought back in touch with her "dark" sexual self, she and Stephen enjoy a marital reconciliation that lasts several months, which culminates in Odalie becoming pregnant with their second child. She is not free of the racism that underpins her identity as a White woman, but she is, literally, pregnant with possibility.

Odalie has begun a process that might lead her, ultimately, to reject the "lenticular logic of racial visibility" discussed earlier. Once she begins to sense possibilities for herself that allow her to reclaim her "dark and sultry passions," she is more able to marry her deeply miscegenated mind with a performance of femininity that is not based on rigid discursive separation (221). One might think of this path as the development of an appositional vision, a term I borrow from the field of entomology that refers to the compound eyes of many insects. Appositional eyes work by gathering images from each lens of the eye and combining them in the brain to create meaning of the insect's world. In this context I use it to highlight the ways in which Odalie's field of vision, so to speak, is expanded such that she can recognize a much broader range of feminine performative possibilities, ones that force her to envision a more complex identity for herself as she works to make sense of her world. Impregnated with possibility for the future—a daughter whom she could free from the misguided and debilitating acceptance of lenticular logic—this belle is truly dangerous to traditional performances of White femininity and, finally, to Whiteness itself.

It is a possibility that Yerby does not think can be born, for the Southern belle who acknowledges the presence of a "little Black blood in her" cannot, ultimately, live (221). Like her female contemporaries of the 1940s, Odalie is required to uphold one vision of what it means to be a White woman, one that expels, not embraces, the darkness (psychological, sexual, and social) within. Consequently and somewhat predictably, within pages of rejecting the bifurcated consciousness that had structured her identity, Odalie dies giving "birth to a stillborn child—a daughter" (237). With her death, both the model of a White female consciousness not wholly wed to racist logics *and* the next generation of women to whom she might pass her subversive understanding of White femininity are exterminated. Further, just before she expires, she also cleanses the White home of Stephen's "dark" distraction by securing his promise that he will "never consort" with his pale mistress, Desiree, again (237). Thus, although interesting for the potential she suggests for white womanhood to liberate itself from the lenticular logic of race and to reproduce Whiteness differently, Odalie ultimately chooses to cling to a false consciousness even into death. Although she embodies the potential for White femininity to reenvision and reimagine itself, it is a journey that Odalie herself never completes.

Clearly the home that Odalie and Stephen create is not ideal. Their marriage is filled with strife and misunderstanding, their union tragically underpinned by their understanding of themselves as raced and gendered subjects. Stephen's understanding of himself as a White man is based on his ability to consume the knowledge, talents, and labor of his slaves without ever admitting to himself or others the real reason for his social ascendancy. As Gwendolyn Foster argues more generally in *Performing Whiteness: Postmodern Re/Constructions in the Cinema*, this unreflective consumption-combined-with-rejection of the racial other is a form of class passing, which, in this particular case, allows Stephen Fox to operate as if it truly is his own ingenuity and self-made luck that have secured for him all of his desires (51). Odalie's performance of Whiteness is based on her unacknowledged reading of how similar her position really is to that of a Black woman in the slaveholding South. Like them, she has only as much choice and freedom as is allowed her within a patriarchal society, and as a result she performs White femininity as an extreme form of physical and emotional control, rejecting human connection as an expression of her autonomy and mastery. This denial and rejection of Blackness on the one hand, and complete dependency on the Africanist presence on the other, makes for a tortured White home. It is not until each of them has been reawakened through Black paramours and sexual midwives, until they embrace the shadow that exists within the White self, that they are able to find happiness, however briefly.

The Foxes of Harrow is an important intervention in and contribution to the cultural conversation about Whiteness, white womanhood, and femininity that was taking place in the 1940s. In many ways, Yerby challenges the basic arguments that were being presented about the social good that would be served by the return of white women to traditional gender roles. *Foxes* presents us with characters who embrace the ideology of Whiteness only to find that it offers them no protection, no satisfaction, no safety, and no home. Their decision to continue investing in Whiteness despite these failures, though, is an important indication of what's at stake for them. As Thandeka, author of *Learning to Be White: Money, Race, and God in America*, reminds us, often the

> emotional content of the term *white* . . . [is] the feeling of being at risk within one's own community because one has committed (or might commit) a communally proscribed act. Such an act threatens emotional perdition: the loss of affection of one's caretakers and/or community of peers. The child and then the adult learn how to suppress such risky feelings of camaraderie with persons beyond the community's racial pale in order to decrease the possibility of being exiled from their own community. (16)

The white woman is shown at a time and place when she is perhaps most revered, but her hold on a socially recognized and socially legitimated subjectivity is tenuous at best and completely dependent on her submission, obedience, and loyalty to the systems of race, class, and gender that structure her society. The White man is supposedly master of all, yet is unable to find domestic harmony unless he is loved and nurtured by black women. To acknowledge or give preference to this, as Stephen almost does on a couple of occasions, puts him at risk of losing family and status in the Creole community, despite his prominence. Although they certainly have privilege associated with their investment in Whiteness, ultimately neither of these characters has any assurance that they would be accepted should they choose to perform a Whiteness that embraces Blackness as a part of itself. Indeed, to retain the esteem of family and community, they each have to close off parts of their humanity to "be White." Thus the

White family is shown to be the source of endless strife and conflict, the White home a space of silence, repression, and denial.

Perhaps Yerby's greatest contribution to our understanding of Whiteness lies in the psychological sketch he offers of Odalie Arceneaux's interior life, the miscegenated mind we see that is always constructing her White identity in rhetorical dialogue with conceptions of Blackness. Here he refuses Whiteness the refuge of thinking of Blackness as something easily identified and contained, something that can be neatly expelled from Whiteness. Rather, Yerby insists on the presence of "Blackness" *within* Whiteness, making the setting of the novel—a New Orleans Creole community—significant. According to Richard A. Long, author of "Creole" in the *Harvard Encyclopedia of American Ethnic Groups*, the term "Creole" initially referred to "Louisianans of French and Spanish descent," an ethnically specific "White" people who sought "to distinguish themselves from the Anglo-Americans who started to move into Louisiana" after the 1803 Louisiana Purchase. But by the twentieth century, Long writes, it "most often refer[red] to the Louisiana Creoles of color," a "self-conscious group" who were the "product of miscegenation in a seigneurial society" (247). Yerby uses this contested attribution of Creole—the fact that it is claimed by both white and black Louisianans as an articulation of identity—as a metaphor for the complexity of White identity itself: the slippage between White and Black, slave and free, marriage and plaçage, self and Other. This move allows Yerby to counter the mythical purity of Whiteness with a vision of Whiteness as a Creolized identity, to highlight the ways that Blackness is always implicated in the emergence of the racially White subject.

Zora Neale Hurston was a wide-ranging, prolific scholar and artist. In her lifetime she published three collections of folklore, four novels, more than twenty-five short stories, several plays (including one cowritten with Langston Hughes), one autobiography, and numerous essays and articles published in journals, magazines, and newspapers. Her subject matter covered everything from ethnographic readings of voodoo and rural Black Southern cultures to Judeo-Christian heritage in the modern world as established through the figure of Moses to rural white life in the early twentieth century. She was a woman with a tremendous and often controversial vision and an insatiable interest in the wide range of humanity and human expression. Although it may be fair to characterize her as an intellectual whose "intellectual life has been given minimal attention," as

Deborah Plant does in her groundbreaking book, *Every Tub Must Sit on Its Own Bottom: The Philosophy and Politics of Zora Neale Hurston*, Hurston is unlike Frank Yerby in one important respect: her work has received sustained attention from the scholarly community since Alice Walker recovered her in the 1970s (2). She has achieved the status of a respected, if not revered, icon of strength, perseverance, and individuality.

Much of the regard Hurston has received as an artist is the result of her persistent engagement with the politics of gender in her work. Many of her novels and short stories, the best regarded of them being *Their Eyes Were Watching God*, feature women who find voice and strength in the face of domineering, sometimes violent, lovers and husbands. Indeed, her commitment to exploring the complexities of women's emotional and psychological lives was an unwavering interest that often yielded profound insights into women's methods of survival, resistance, and self-fashioning. Likewise, Hurston's biography itself seems to evidence a woman navigating those issues in her own life, a woman determined to find a space that would enable her to follow the path that she envisioned for herself at a time when the opportunities open to women, and in particular black women, were severely circumscribed. She pursued education, completing a degree in anthropology from Barnard University under the tutelage of Franz Boas; and she married, and divorced, three husbands in her search for a partner who would accept her as an equal and not limit her autonomy. Given all of this, it remains an intriguing fact that many of Hurston's writings have ambiguous endings for the female protagonists, such as the conclusion of *Eyes* wherein Janie retires to her room, possibly dying, to relive her time with Tea Cake. Compounding even further the apparent contradictions between her political and personal definition of a successful heterosexual union and the representations of those relationships in her art, are statements like the one she wrote to Burroughs Mitchell, her editor at Scribner's: "You know yourself that a woman is most powerful when she is weak. . . . All a woman needs to have is sufficient allure, and able men will move the world for her" (Hurston, *Life in Letters*, 562). Here, in typical Hurston fashion, she seems to dance between an *analysis* of women's power in a patriarchal culture and a *prescription* for a feminine performance that enables women to access power in a system set up to benefit others. All of these facets of Hurston's life and writings, combined with the ambivalent outcomes her female characters often face, have led Deborah Plant to conclude, "In spite of an expressed concern with the lack of equanimity in traditional female-male relationships, Hurston never articulated a true complementary relationship of mutual respect and equal power sharing" (166). Complexities like these have only fueled academic interest in Hurston as an artist and a personality.

Hurston is also celebrated, of course, because of her sustained interest in exploring and representing black lives and culture. Her interest in African American culture first became evident in the anthropological fieldwork she pursued, collecting folk stories among rural black people in the United States and the Caribbean. That work was the basis of her first two publications, *Mules and Men* and *Tell My Horse*, which earned her recognition and then status as an insider in the "New Negro" movement, which would later be known as the Harlem Renaissance. However, the regard she received was eroded by continuous and harsh criticisms of her personal politics and professional work; eventually, her interest in lower-class black life and women's experiences seemed out of step with the agenda makers of the Harlem Renaissance, people like W. E. B. Du Bois and Alain Locke, who believed in a "talented tenth" who would speak for the uneducated Black masses. Additionally, while many of her contemporaries sought the full recognition and participation of blacks in American society, Hurston espoused sociopolitical positions that did not seem to support an integration agenda. In fact, she believed completely in the value of an autonomous, perhaps even "authentic" black culture, and feared that a whitewashing of African American culture might result from integration and the demands of assimilation. The distance between Hurston and prominent African American intellectuals of her time grew, even as Hurston became more aware that much of her writing, especially the collections of folklore, was being used to support prevailing attitudes and beliefs about the primitivism of Black Americans. She had sought to present an alternative view of Black life that dramatized its resilience, integrity, and self-sufficiency, but she knew all too well the compromises she had made to get her work published—from the uneasy patronage she received from Charlotte Osgood Mason to the writing of her own, heavily revised autobiography. By the 1940s, although she continued to have significant relationships with and support from white artists, intellectuals, editors, and patrons, she had serious reason to doubt the ability of her work to make a difference in society (West, 204). Further, her own words and beliefs about American racism were being misrepresented, as in the case of an interview she granted to the *New York World Telegram* in 1943. There, she was quoted as saying "the Jim Crow system works," a charge she denied in letters to her interviewer, Douglas Gilbert, as well as to friends (Hemenway, 289). "Nothing has ever upset me so much as this printed thing with Douglas Gilbert. It is so untrue, so twisted!" she wrote to Claude Barnett (*Life in Letters*, 474). She ended her note to him,

> But one thing is definite. The iron has entered my soul. Since my god of tolerance has forsaken me, I am ready for anything to overthrow Anglo-Saxon supremacy, however desperate. I have become what I never wished to be, a good hater. I no longer even value my life if by losing it, I can do something to destroy this Anglo-Saxon monstrosity. (475)

Five years later, *Seraph on the Suwanee* was published.

Seraph is the story of a White family living in post–Reconstruction era Florida. The protagonist, Arvay Henson Meserve, is a lower-class woman who finds herself entangled with the ambitious, determined, and formerly well-established newcomer Jim Meserve. Their courtship ends and marriage begins with Arvay's rape, and she spends most of the rest of the novel trying simultaneously to accept and resist her rapist/husband's goals for their lives. She is painfully insecure and timid, an outsider in her own home, and yet she becomes not only the "proper wife" to the accomplished patriarch of the family but also the epitome of an upper-class White woman. Genevieve West argues in her book *Zora Neale Hurston and American Literary Culture* that writing about White characters liberated Hurston from "criticisms that she exploited lower-class Black life for White readers," and other scholars have suggested that Hurston published a white life novel for primarily pecuniary reasons (204). Both of these explanations are likely accurate, but there is an even more intriguing possibility: that long-time insider and close compatriot to White America, Zora Neale Hurston, wrote *Seraph* because she had something to say about Whiteness.

Critical readings of *Seraph on the Suwanee*, as few as they are, have largely dismissed this novel as deeply flawed, the result of a misapplication of Hurston's talent. Robert Hemenway gave full voice to this critical assessment of *Seraph* in his *Zora Neale Hurston: A Literary Biography*, asserting that Hurston "largely turned her back on the source of her creativity" in writing a novel about White characters (307). In another influential piece, entitled "A Woman Half in Shadows," Mary Helen Washington writes, "All of the main characters in *Seraph* are white, and, apparently, Zora wrote this strange book to prove that she was capable of writing about white people. The intent may have been admirable, but . . . the result is an awkward and contrived novel, as vacuous as a soap opera" (136). Not until 1989 did a significant shift occur in the critical approaches to *Seraph on the Suwanee*. That year, Janet St. Clair published "The Courageous Undertow of Zora Neale Hurston's *Seraph on the Suwanee*," wherein she identified a "subversive subtext" to the novel, a reevaluation that began a slow shift in the scholarly tide as others were emboldened to challenge the Hurston-abandons-black-subjects approach to the novel (40). Over the next decade, several more scholars examined *Seraph* in new and compelling ways, including Ann duCille, who noted that Hurston had engaged the gender politics of the "coupling convention" more fully in *Seraph* than in any of her other works. Freed from concerns of activating the mythology of the Black male rapist through the use of white characters, Hurston offers, according to duCille, "an anatomical dissection of the psychosexual daily dramas and dilemmas of the marital here and now," including the naming of marital rape as a reality that women had to make sense of (124).

Only two scholars, Laura Dubek and Chuck Jackson, have examined Whiteness as a theme that makes a difference in Hurston's last novel. Dubek's "The Social Geography of Race in Hurston's *Seraph on the Suwanee*" examines the ways in which the "social position" of the main character, Arvay Henson Meserve, is "circumscribed by race, class, and gender—intersecting forces of both privilege and oppression" (341). Noting that scholarship has traditionally assumed that "it is people of color, not white, who live racially structured lives," Dubek goes on to demonstrate the ways in which Arvay's life is defined on the one hand by her Whiteness and the privilege that it affords her, and on the other by class and gender that tend to undermine her racial privilege (342). Ultimately, she argues, "Hurston constructs Arvay's whiteness, then, as a shield that encloses but does not protect, as a blinding force that, together with class and despite gender, enables one woman to construct a self-image by denying human status to poor whites and people of color" (343–344). Jackson focuses on the theme of cleanliness in his "Waste and Whiteness: Zora Neale Hurston and the Politics of Eugenics," arguing for a connection between Arvay's "white trash identity" and "narratives of anthropological eugenics" that were popular from 1900 into the 1940s (641). Demonstrating that "eugenics worries the relation between the private white body and the public, social body of whiteness," Jackson concludes that *Seraph* "is about waste and whiteness, an (at times) winking critique of white paranoias about personal and social purity" (645, 656). What Jackson and

Dubek share is a dedication to excavating the meanings and implications of Whiteness, both individual and social, that are suggested in Hurston's novel. They assume, as I do, that the creation of white characters by African American artists *can be* about more than simply flexing one's writerly muscles or trying to gain acceptance in a white literary landscape. Hurston, the notoriously observant, trained anthropologist, saw something when she turned her critical gaze and expressive prowess upon poor, White, Southern women: Whiteness as a racial category and social identity that was constructed and maintained in the White home. She recognized that the same power that defined interactions across the color line also animated gender relations within Whiteness, and she posited that the social mobility of White women was premised upon their investment in Whiteness even more than a particular understanding of their "place" as women. When writing about White women's lives, Hurston permitted herself to comment on "race" in ways that she had rarely expressed in her work on Black subjectivities.

Seraph is a novel that complicates the idea of the ideal White woman at a very fundamental level. Arvay Henson Meserve is not a conventional, refined heroine when she is first introduced in the narrative. She is poor and poorly educated, and clings tenaciously to her identity as a "Florida Cracker." Instead of showing genteel, lady-like largess and poise, Arvay is miserly, petty, and often ill tempered. Instead of being self-assured, she feels unloved and unseen, and lacks self-confidence. Perhaps for these reasons as much as out of a commitment to racist ideologies, Arvay "cling[s] to the conviction that Whiteness is a source of security and superiority" (Powdermaker, 25). It becomes a means of mitigating her insecurity, and even as she moves literally from Sawley to Citrabelle, which represents a figurative move into a middle-class, then upper-class socioeconomic status, her habit of elevating her own sense of self by denigrating racialized Others remains intact. Arvay is also a fervent Christian, but like the image of the Southern belle discussed earlier, her religiosity does not portend a strong moral center and ability to guide others toward ethical action. Rather, it disguises a secret life of adulterous longing for her brother-in-law. Hurston's heroine is anything but a lady born and bred. Arvay's journey to respectable, upper-class womanhood provides a lesson in what women have to suppress, deny, and endure in order to conform to the image of the mythic White lady. Arvay's transformation allows us to explore the imbrications between race, gender, and class in the performance of White femininity and in the construction of the white home, both of which were being offered as the route back to American cultural ascendancy in the 1940s.

By juxtaposing Arvay and Jim's socialization around gender and race from the beginning, Hurston calls attention to the interdependence of their performances of race and gender. Like Arvay, Jim Meserve is entangled and defined by the choices he has available to him for navigating the nexus of race, class, and gender, and, like his wife, he is discouraged from recognizing the ways in which race and class structure his performance of masculinity. From the time he enters the town of Sawley, Jim is regarded as different from, and better than, the locals. Sawley is characterized by "ignorance and poverty, and the ever-present hookworm" (*Seraph*, 1). The yards and farms are littered with "scratchy plantings" and "scanty flowers," and the people live off the land because "none of it cost you a cent" (2). Jim is associated with ingenuity and progress; he is "White" in ways that they are not, and his status establishes both internal and external expectations for his success. Indeed, the expectations are so great that even when Jim has nothing and knows nothing about the local industries that will help him earn back the fortune his family lost in the Civil War, he is regarded as superior, a "good catch." He is ambitious and determined, but, much like Yerby's Stephen Fox, Jim accomplishes his economic and social elevation by colonizing the knowledge, ingenuity, and labor of people of color. His race and social class, though, prevent onlookers from recognizing his dependency or vulnerability. Consequently, he is expected to conquer his resistant love interest, Arvay, and to succeed in "breaking her" where other, lesser men have failed. In fact, he hangs his reputation on securing her as his wife through a very public courtship and several public pronouncements to that effect. Ironically, though, even this success is not completely his own. He must consult the African American laborer Joe Kelsey for advice.[10]

The relationship that evolves between Arvay and Jim is fraught with conflict, misunderstanding, and mistrust. The strife begins, as several critics have noted, with the traumatic rape that binds Arvay to Jim in marriage. Already insecure, the rape brings back "all her old feelings of defeat and inadequacy," and from this moment, the spunky woman who once feigned religious fits to preserve a space of autonomy for herself basically vanishes (51). The Arvay that moves forward in the story is a woman who thinks of herself as homeless even as she constructs a home; who seems to react to rather than engage with the powerful social constructions of gender, race, and class that circumscribe her; and who feels powerless even as she participates in intricate, daily negotiations of power within her home and community. As Dubek accurately argues, Arvay does not recognize "race and racism as factors that shape her environment and determine her individual identity" (341). But what is perhaps most interesting about this narrative is not the fact that Arvay doesn't see race; many critical race scholars have noted that part of the power of Whiteness lies is its ability to remain unnamed, invisible, and "natural." What is noteworthy is that she *does see* class, despite sociocultural disincentives that are at least as strong as the disincentives for whites to recognize racism as the foundation of American society. In fact, she is acutely aware of the ways that class shapes her experience, both in terms of the expectations for class-based behavior and attitudes as well as in terms of what she has to relinquish of her (lower-class) self in order to perform upper-class White femininity in socially acceptable ways. That she actively resists the process of socialization that would allow her to embrace her rising class status is the source of continual conflict in her marriage: the more she clings to her identity as a "Florida Cracker," the more she is set apart from, and often set against, her husband. But she never extends that critical eye to any other facet of her identity, perhaps evidencing a willed ignorance around issues of race that allows her to benefit from the racialized thinking of the community without engaging the "personal incoherence" that James Baldwin spoke of in his essay "White Man's Guilt" (411). Hurston, then, is certainly examining the blindnesses and silences that enable Whiteness, highlighting the "connection between the social construction of White womanhood and economic and racial structures of oppression" (Dubek, 344). However, I believe that Hurston is also locating her interrogation of race, class, gender, and white womanhood much more squarely in the analysis of power relations than has heretofore been recognized. Power is the answer to the question of the novel: How does a lower-class woman come to embrace the very systems that oppress her so that she can be recognized as a White lady?

Michel Foucault, while certainly not the first to analyze power, is the intellectual most often credited for recognizing that power can never be exercised or established absolutely.[11] Power, like all other systems of authority, is a force that is continually asserted, negotiated, and reinscribed according to parameters that are constantly mediated by and within a society. Power moves. Even the oppressed can find or create spaces in which they are able to exercise power: to challenge the control of their oppressors, to awaken public sentiment and change the course of public discourse, or to redefine the very terms by which their positioning is justified. It is by acknowledging that power is not absolute that we are able to recognize and account for the complex positioning of many marginalized groups, like African American men who are traditionally disadvantaged in American society because of their race and the racialized stereotypes used to define their masculinity, but who also enjoy certain privileges vis-à-vis their gender in a patriarchal society. Another example of the movement and negotiation of power occurred during the Harlem Renaissance, when African American artists and intellectuals found their work being celebrated and supported by white Americans. Often these artists used their influence to advance the conversations and causes of equality among the dominant group, but they also felt pressure to compromise their vision so that it would be more palatable to that very audience, raising questions about how to retain creative control over their work while making it appeal to a wider range of consumers. In writing *Seraph on the Suwanee*, Hurston, who wrote candidly about these very issues in two essays, "The Rise of the Begging Joints" (1945) and "What White Publishers Won't Print" (1950), turns her attention from the pendulum of power that Black America has historically had to navigate to the nexus of power that enlivens white women's understanding of their racial and gendered identities. What she sees when she shifts her focus is a practiced and carefully orchestrated movement between subordination and domination in which white women embrace their subjugation vis-à-vis the culturally dominant White male by asserting White racial privilege over racial and social "non-Whites," a subconscious psychological dance that resembles nothing so much as the social and psychological drama of sadomasochism.

Popular culture largely understands S&M as consensual erotic role play in which one partner dominates the other for mutual sexual pleasure. The iconic representation of this coupling is that of an attractive, leather-stiletto-and-whip-clad woman standing suggestively over a bound but obviously satisfied man. She, the sadist, is in control and relishing her power; he, the masochist, is at her mercy but enjoying his powerlessness, the control he has relinquished to her. This popular representation of sadomasochistic coupling plays with our expectations of successful relationships by inverting traditional gender roles that situate women as weak, helpless, and subordinate, men as strong and in control. Largely ignored is the fact that at the end of the sexual role-play, the man returns to his corporate life of control and his social dominance in the home; that the formerly empowered dominatrix settles back into a relatively disempowered position in relation to her dominant male partner is also disregarded. The eroticization of these positions masks the complex negotiation of power at work in these relationships. This simultaneous process of, on the one hand, eroticizing the experience of power and, on the other, masking the exercise of power makes domination and subordination seem not only natural but also desirable.

According to Suzanne Gearhart, however, the mechanisms by which "inequality, subordination, humiliation, or pain" are transformed from "an experience of displeasure" into "a source of pleasure" are themselves worth analysis; this was a topic in which Foucault was deeply interested (Gearhart, 391). Lynne Chancer, author of *Sadomasochism in Everyday Life*, perhaps first suggested this direction for the study of power in interpersonal relationships when she asserted that sadomasochism "may be more generally distributed than rare, and at once sociologically and psychologically rooted, in capitalist, racialized and male-dominant societies that are rife with overlapping inequities" ("Rethinking," 257). Both scholars emphasize the fact that a single person can be placed in both sadistic and masochistic positions at different moments, perhaps even within the same moment, and that there is pleasure attached to the exercise (and experience, Foucault would argue) of power. Focusing on white womanhood, *Seraph* seems to suggest another layer to this rather abstract analysis of power: the ways in which movement between the positions of sadist and masochist can be used to constitute an easily identifiable social identity vis-à-vis race and gender. Hurston demonstrates that the performance of White femininity is linked to the white woman's ability to capitalize on the movement of power within and among a number of asymmetrical power relationships that exist in the White home.

To begin, it is important to recognize that Hurston is not representing a prearranged, carefully thought out S&M relationship. The Meserves are not intentionally taking on the roles of sadist and masochist, nor do they recognize the complex matrix of power that penetrates and defines their home and family. Rather, the dynamic at work in their marriage is a result of their socialization, the ways in which domination and submission have been eroticized and naturalized in their society. They are simply following the typical coupling conventions, to borrow duCille's incisive phrasing, that govern heterosexual matches at the turn of the twentieth century, conventions that have taught them to expect an unequal distribution of power in marriage with the male being dominant. This message of dominance and subordination is compounded and reinforced by the fact that Arvay and Jim identify with different socioeconomic classes, another area of interaction often defined by hierarchical power relations. These factors combine to disempower Arvay and to press upon her the depth of her inferiority, and to impress upon Jim his "natural" superiority and right to dominance. A decade into their coupling, however, there is clear evidence that the social impetuses toward sadism and masochism have matured into a more profound S&M interaction in the Meserve marriage, which has profound implications for how Arvay understands her options for feminine performance and identity.

One scene that reveals the progress of this dynamic within their marriage occurs when Jim and Arvay travel to see their son, Kenny, perform at a college football game. For one of the first times, Arvay makes her desire (to leave the game) clear and refuses to let Jim bully her into changing her mind. As Chancer's work predicts of real-life S&M relationships, Arvay's assertion of will has immediate and "severe repercussions" because she has challenged the power of her sadist husband (Chancer, *Sadomasochism*, 3). If the challenge is not immediately countered and Jim's power reasserted, their relationship will be in danger of expiring because the roles have been irrevocably overturned: the masochist will have discovered her own power. Sensing the possibility of her strength, Arvay says, "I think too much of myself to kill you like I ought to, but I'm through with you Jim Meserve. I'm just as through with you as I is my baby-shirt." Jim responds to this threat explosively, with psychological and physical assaults upon Arvay designed to demean and humiliate her into submission once again. In order to undermine her burgeoning self-confidence and assertiveness, he has to reestablish her inalienable desire for and need to be with him; she has to be made to doubt her strength once again. He begins by flinging her into their bedroom, then screaming at her, threatening to beat her, and reminding her that she is his "damn property" (*Seraph*, 215–216). He orders her to undress and, when she refuses, forcibly strips her and forces her to stand naked before him. While several critics have commented upon Jim's violence and callousness in this scene, Arvay's response to his abuse has gone unmentioned. While desperate to regain his approval and the affection she believes she has compromised, she, significantly, also becomes sexually aroused. Her breathing changes, her temperature rises, and a "greenish infusion" creeps into her eyes, the latter being a symbol of her sexual arousal throughout the text. After more than ten years with Jim, Arvay's emotional suffering and physical discomfort are now coded psychologically as sources of (sexual) pleasure for her. Her conversion to a masochistic subject position in her marriage is complete.

Jim forces Arvay's submission, as he does repeatedly throughout the novel, to affirm his masculine dominance in their marriage. But these gendered performances are intimately connected to the Meserves' understanding of their racial identity, for Jim's sense of himself as a powerful and dominant White man is inextricably bound to Arvay's performance as a weak, dependent, adoring wife—the ideal of upper-class White femininity. The domestic space they create is one that mirrors the public expectation of acceptable gender roles, and rather than marginalizing them, the sadomasochistic exchanges that structure Jim and Arvay's union signify their insider status in Whiteness. His ability to tame and elevate his resistant lover is what marks Jim as masterful, and this sadomasochistic dynamic is also what motivates Arvay to accept Jim's performance of Whiteness as the standard she must achieve.

But Whiteness is neither monolithic nor natural in *Seraph*. Rather, Hurston presents a picture of Whiteness that is diverse, contested, and even coerced. As was the case in *Foxes*, it is an identity that depends on conceptions of Blackness, or more broadly "coloredness," to make meaning of itself. For Arvay's lower-class background, this dialectic has been figured almost exclusively in terms of distance from Blackness; the mere fact of her Whiteness became the element of her identity that allowed her to mitigate another distance, that which existed between her experience as "White trash" and dominant cultural constructions of Whiteness as economically secure and socially and culturally elevated. Hurston, however, repeatedly illustrates in this text that establishing rigid racial and cultural boundaries is a tenuous basis for white racial identity, for the economic and social elevation of white people is often predicated on close proximity to—not distance from—African Americans. At the turn of the twentieth century, African American labor enriched White men, and the presence and service of African American domestic workers helped to define the White middle class (home). Constructions of African American sexuality were used to limn out White masculinity, and as Grace Elizabeth Hale has insightfully suggested, these same gender constructions enabled the paradox of White femininity: "White women empowered by an image of weakness" (105). In the politics of the United States at the turn of the twentieth century (and to the present), class mobility and White supremacy were built upon the actual and symbolic presence of African Americans.[12] This is a lesson that Jim Meserve, formally of the upper classes himself, has

already internalized, and as the Meserves continue to reinforce their economic security, he challenges Arvay to show a similar paternalistic largess
toward those Othered by race/ethnicity and economic positioning. It is,
however, a difficult Whiteness to perform for one not socialized into it.
Arvay recognizes that being the woman Jim wants requires her to deny
something of her past and her learned racial practices; to hold them, even,
in disdain. In response to demands and expectations of this sort, Arvay
clings more stubbornly to her "Cracker" identity as a space of resistance.
She also identifies more closely with her racialized, first-born son, Earl
David Meserve.

As both Dubek and Jackson have pointed out, the character of Earl
Meserve is interesting for the analysis of racialized masculinity that he
makes possible. As his first description makes clear, something is not quite
right about Earl:

> There was practically no forehead nor backhead on her child. The head
> narrowed like an egg on top. . . . The feet were long, and the toes well
> formed, but they looked too long for a new-born baby to have. And there
> was no arch to the tiny feet. They were perfectly flat, with a little lump of
> flesh huddled under what should have been the instep. . . . [The mouth] was
> exceptionally small, and what there was of it was concentrated in the bottom
> lip. (*Seraph*, 68).

From his ill-formed head to his flat feet to his protruding lip, Earl is
described in terms typically reserved for African Americans. His is a
deformed White body that does not fit classical images of Whiteness or
reflect mastery and perfection.[13] He is also basically mute and believed
incapable of intelligence and self-direction, again defying the social expectations for white masculinity. In fact, the only "evidence" of his capacity
for thought is his cunning and ability to mislead, aligning him squarely
with nineteenth-century stereotypes of black masculinity. Earl wants to
lay claim to his father's power nonetheless, a mastery that is denied him
because he is "less than White." Jackson argues that "Earl's deformed white
body" and inability to "use language properly to define himself in relation
to others" makes it impossible for him to "carve out a normative white
subjectivity" (648), while Dubek focuses on the community's response to
Earl when he is seen to have enacted "a violent and unacceptable transgression of fixed racial boundaries" (348). Both of these readings point
to Earl's close association with Blackness. But they also fail to read Earl

within the context of the familial drama that is *Seraph on the Suwanee*. It is within that context, I believe, that we can understand most fully Earl's significance to the narrative and to Hurston's analysis of race and power.

The similarities between the actions and aspirations of the eldest Meserve son and his father, Jim, are striking. First, both refuse to accept their social positioning as intractable. Jim seeks to regain wealth lost during the Civil War and to reestablish himself not only as a social elite but also as an entrepreneur and financial tycoon. Earl refuses his designation as a failed heir to the Meserve legacy and attempts to usurp the power of the father by killing Jim. Additionally, both father and son rely on violence to assert their will. Jim secures Arvay as his wife through brutality and sexual terror while Earl attempts to do the same through his feral attack on Lucy Ann Corregio. But whereas Jim is able to legitimize his rape of Arvay because he has the socially sanctioned power to define what constitutes sexual violation, Earl does not have the voice or power to redefine his assault. He is cast in the narrative as a violent, lascivious beast (read: Black rapist), and a White male mob is organized to hunt him down, a powerful indication of how far from White he is considered. And whereas Jim has the tacit and explicit support of other White men in the community who respect and aspire to his position, Earl is isolated and without a community of supporters who want to see themselves in him. The rage of the White mob unifies them and aligns them against Earl, who, as a failed "cacogenic" specimen, is expulsed from the public body of Whiteness (Jackson, 648); they destroy his all-too-visible degeneracy. Much like the violent rituals that Trudier Harris describes in *Exorcising Blackness: Historical and Literary Lynching and Burning Rituals*, Jim uses Earl's death, which is suggestively reminiscent of a lynching party, to usher in a public display of grief, mourning, and closure. Thus, the younger Meserve is the vehicle for exorcising the personal demons of Arvay's and Jim's past and the public memory of their humble beginnings. Earl's death erases the only "evidence" in the text that the Whiteness of the Meserve clan is learned and performed rather than being an inalienable, biological characteristic. His demise enables a metamorphosis of the Meserve family into a mythical Whiteness.

After the death of her son, which symbolically is the death of her not-quite-right Whiteness, and many more years of marital strife during which Arvay consistently complains that Jim places more emphasis on the desires of his laborers than he does her wishes, Jim leaves their relationship and gives Arvay a year to decide whether she wants to remain in the marriage. She returns to her childhood community of Sawley, fully intending to continue her life as a single, independent woman. While there, she becomes acutely aware of the comforts she had enjoyed in her life with Jim Meserve: she is well dressed, well provided for, and deferred to as a social elite by others in the community. Although previously resistant to her social elevation as Mrs. Meserve, she now becomes cognizant of the distance she has traveled from her impoverished beginnings and the power she has at her disposal. She returns to her comfortable residence in Citrabelle determined to embrace her position as an upper-class lady. She becomes more assertive and exercises more control in her home, fully realizing and accessing the privilege she has as a racial and social elite and the authority she has as a result of her husband's status. It is in this shift from feeling powerless to recognizing herself as powerful that we can come to understand the complex motivations that have driven Arvay throughout the novel. Clinging to her lower-class, "Cracker" identity was her way of preserving a sense of superiority in an environment in which she felt unseen and unheard. Her resistance was not only evidence of her insecurity and uneasiness with her new role as Mrs. Meserve but also an investment in seeing the White self—*her* White self—as superior. Thus, once she recognizes herself as privileged in another area of her life, she willingly subjugates herself to her husband, playing the demure and adoring coquette to his performance of dominant masculinity. Hurston reveals a powerful connection between these two positions that Arvay embraces in her performance of upper-class femininity. Arvay no longer resents or resists the excessive dependence she is forced to experience in her marriage because she is able to inhabit the role of dominant masochist in her relationships with economic and racial Others. Indeed, it is because she exercises so little power in her marriage that she chafed at the lack of control she also felt in relation to servants and laborers in the home. Once she is able to make the connection between the two performances of femininity, however, she is able to accept her "new identity." Thus, Hurston demonstrates that the White middle-class home, with its plethora of lower-class and "colored" servants, is the space where traditional White femininity is not only enacted but also enabled. Arvay's socialization into mythical Whiteness is only possible in a space where she can assert racial and economic supremacy as a compensation for the masochistic position expected of her as an elite White woman.

The denouement of *Seraph* is one that critics have struggled to make sense of, but I believe that the key to it lies in understanding the pendulum of power that Hurston has exposed in the lives of white women. In the novel's ending, after twenty years of strife, the Meserves reconcile in spectacular fashion—sailing through a turbulent ocean pass aboard Jim's shrimping boat, named the Arvay Henson (Arvay's maiden name). After making it safely through the pass in a scene meant to symbolize a new birth for their marriage, Arvay completely embraces her identity as wife, mother, and servant to her family while Jim sleeps peacefully in her arms. Hurston's exploration of the interconnections among race, gender, class, and power in this White home has led us to one conclusion: that the deepest desire of the partners in a sadomasochistically structured relationship is not the complete enactment of either the sadist's or the masochist's role. Jim's primary complaint about their marriage is that Arvay does not acknowledge his efforts to provide for her and their family. By the end, however, it becomes clear that the source of Jim's frustration is that Arvay's attitudes and actions effectively prohibited him from relinquishing the dominant role he had secured in the marriage through his bullying and violence. He was always forced to wear the guise of masculinity and mastery, in public as well as private, as opposed to being able to transform himself, to be "someone else," when not on display. The pressure Jim feels to perform this dominant role is directly tied to his racial identity. His Whiteness (as opposed to Arvay's, for instance) is always in view, always visible, even though it masquerades as the norm and is thereby seemingly made less visible. As a white man who has worked hard to erase his family's humble, "non-White" beginnings, Jim must maintain his public performance of Whiteness at all times lest he risk the loss of status that could accompany a public "slip" of his facade. Consequently, he tries to assume a less dominant role on occasion, to create a space where he can lay down his power without relinquishing it. Indeed, Jim all but acknowledges this latent desire on one occasion when he admits to himself that something "reached to him and delivered him into her hands tied and bound." And although he does not "consider himself weak in being overcome like that," he decides not to let Arvay know the power she has over him for fear that it might irrevocably transform their relationship (*Seraph*, 105–106). In other words, Jim fears that he will lose his sadistic power over Arvay should she ever discover his deep and uncontrollable need for her. What he wants is the ability to maintain sadistic control even when he has relinquished that *role* for a while—an occasional, nonbinding transformation of himself within the relationship, not of the power dynamics of the relationship itself.

As for Arvay, there are clearly instances in which she appears to abdicate her power in favor of a more submissive role with her husband. In these moments, she chooses to remain in a masochistic position even though on some level she knows she has the strength to stand alone. She first exhibits her power when she turns away suitor after suitor by feigning religious fits in order to maintain some control over her own destiny. She once again accesses this self-determination when she returns to Sawley for a time and then decides to reconcile with her husband. The Arvay that returns to Jim, however, seems anything but contrite and timid. Rather, she boldly engages in playful banter and teasing with her husband, realizing that after twenty years, "She was not the only one who had trembled. All these years and time, Jim had been feeling his way towards her and grasping at her as she had been towards him." Arvay finally recognizes the power and control that she has over her husband—his most guarded secret—which transforms her into a more dominant partner than she had previously been. She remains outwardly submissive to him but is aware that this stance is just a role that she plays for the benefit of Jim and their relationship. This new understanding infuses her with strength, and she immediately determines "not [to] let him know what she had perceived." Instead, she looks up, "innocently afraid and scared," in order that Jim might retain his vision of himself as the dominant partner (348). Importantly, hers is a power that she cannot openly relish. At the moment she recognizes it, she immediately acts out the role of passive femininity that Jim and society have demanded of her. Yet this secure and confident Arvay is not compromised by the role-playing or her apparently submissive position within the marriage. Rather, her ability to manipulate the power dynamics of her marriage and, to a lesser extent, her husband, is ultimately offered as her final glory. It is only when Arvay is able control people and events around her with skill and precision while appearing not to that her feelings of illegitimacy and homelessness are finally resolved. It is only when she masters the ability to participate in these complex matrices of power *while appearing to have an aversion to the exercise of power* that she becomes seamlessly and unassailably a "White lady."

For Arvay and Jim Meserve, the boundaries between the personal and the public, the domestic and the political, are permeable. Indeed, it is precisely because the sociopolitical systems of the United States are so defined by hierarchical conceptions of race, gender, and class that the private life of the Meserves is also structured by these schemas of dominance and subordination. But it is a cycle that does not end with their relationship.

These internalized sadomasochistic dramas begin to play themselves out in the relationships that Arvay has with her subordinates as she seeks spaces in which she can be more autonomous and assertive. Her interactions are essentially an emotional demand that they recognize her *racially located power*, which is, ultimately, the power she is structurally granted in a racist patriarchy. Thus Hurston suggests that this complex psychological balance between power and disempowerment, between dominance and subordination, is what structures the psychology of White women.

At a time when the United States was heavily invested in an ideology of the "[White] hearthside angel," as Janet St. Clair succinctly described the construction, both Frank Yerby and Zora Neale Hurston sensed an opportunity to challenge America's assumptions about the White home as an apolitical, safe space for White women (39). Both suggest ways of reading that focus on the exercises of power needed to maintain race, class, and gender hierarchies in the United States. They subverted popular romantic storylines like the one presented in *Gone with the Wind*[14] by unmasking the "making" of the proper White lady and laying bare the negotiations of power that enable and sustain the White home and family. Rather than presenting a romanticized view of White femininity as politically disengaged and encircled by adoring "darkies" who respect the cultural positions of the white woman and home, these two authors inundate us with images of sexual violence and coercion within the White home; White colonization of black ingenuity skating thinly over an Africanist presence poised to challenge White supremacy; and understandings of White femininity that are anything but free of the politics of race, class, and navigations of power. By demonstrating that White femininity was a matter of socialization and performance, both Yerby and Hurston deconstructed claims that white women's return to the domestic sphere was somehow a return to a "natural" and intended order. The White home became politicized.

They each also offered a unique perspective on the cultural conversation about white womanhood and femininity that was raging during the 1940s. Yerby's analysis focuses on the issue of how race impacts the construction of white feminine identity. Countering contemporary arguments that effectively sought to continue the displacement of African Americans from the sociopolitical enterprise of America, *The Foxes of Harrow* presents a subversive narrative of a Whiteness that is always already enmeshed in Blackness, a Creolized identity in which racial "mixing" is unavoidable because it takes place within White psychology. The fact that women are not immune to this intellectual and emotional amalgamation, even if they are unconscious of the ways in which "Blackness" shapes their psyche, means that White purity is a fantasy and a lie. Hurston's narrative, on the other hand, highlights the negotiations and navigations of power required to maintain both Whiteness and the White home. In giving voice to the lower-class white community that was so often repressed and denied within mainstream popular culture, she sought to complicate America's vision of Whiteness, to "dirty" the dominant images of White refinement, success, and purity. Calling attention to the uneasy politics of White socioeconomic mobility and subverting the mythology of the White home as apolitical, *Seraph on the Suwanee* focuses on the pendulous movement between dominance and subordination, the sadomasochistic exchanges that enable Jim and Arvay to perform race and gender in ways that make them more at home in Whiteness. Indeed, these navigations of power are ultimately what allow the couple to successfully class pass.

As white womanhood was being offered as the panacea through which Whiteness could be rebuilt and reified around a stable image of cultural superiority, both Yerby and Hurston offered complex explorations of White female subjectivity. The picture that emerges in each is of a nuanced subjectivity that is immersed in and shaped by—not immune from—the sociopolitical realities of the United States. Well before critical race theory's or feminism's sustained engagement with questions of racial identity, or the critical recognition of (White) racial myopia, these novels provided critical insights into the interconnections of Whiteness, class, and gender identities. These novels represent a long road traveled within the literature of white estrangement. Whereas early considerations of white womanhood effectively absolved white women of any responsibility for the oppressiveness of Whiteness, these authors explored the complicated and often unconscious investment White women have in maintaining Whiteness.

Chapter Three

"OCCUPIED TERRITORY"

Mapping the Spatial Geographies
of White Identity and Violence

The white man is more afraid of separation than he is of integration.
—Malcolm X, "The Ballot or the Bullet"

In silence, we have spent our years watching the ofays, trying to understand them, on the principle that you have a better chance coping with
the known than with the unknown. Some of us have been, and some
still are, interested in learning whether it is *ultimately* possible to live in
the same territory with people who seem so disagreeable to live with.
—Eldridge Cleaver, *Soul on Ice*

To travel, I must always move through fear, confront terror.
—bell hooks, "Representations of Whiteness in the Black Imagination"

If the word *integration* means anything, this is what it means:
that we, with love, shall force our brothers to see themselves as
they are, to cease fleeing from reality and begin to change it.
—James Baldwin, *The Fire Next Time*

In 1954, the United States Supreme Court ruled in *Brown v. Board of Education* that segregation in public schools was illegal, overturning fifty-
eight years of legal support for the policy of "separate but equal."[1] Three
years later—and only a few years before images of attack dogs, fire hoses,
bombed structures, and the uninhibited force of racial brutality would
become commonplace in American civic and political consciousness—
schools in many Southern communities, including Little Rock, Arkansas,

103

were in the early stages of implementing plans that would desegregate institutions of learning from the primary grades through postsecondary levels. Against this backdrop, the battle to desegregate Central High School in Little Rock was set. It came to national attention when the governor, Orval Faubus, took decisive action to preserve segregation in Arkansas schools. His stand to prevent nine African American students, who would become known as the Little Rock Nine, from entering Central High energized Southern segregationists; the resistance to integration became more organized, more vocal, and more strident in the wake of Faubus's stance.[2] Images of an irate mob of girls and women pursuing a lone African American child, a fully armed Arkansas National Guard unit aligned to prevent the entry of African Americans to the school, and federal troops on maneuvers in the community soon framed the discourse surrounding racism (largely read here as racism in the South) and the African American demand for civil rights. In the photos and film of this iconic confrontation, Central High's massive structure is invoked if not included. Its large and imposing facade, which stood in stark contrast to the numerous "Negro schools" in the community which were much smaller, older, and, predictably, not as well equipped, became emblematic of all that African Americans had to overcome and all that was at stake if concerted efforts at social change were not successful. Thus, Central became not only the physical location of the battle to desegregate but also, as an ideological battleground, the symbolic hub of a contentious confrontation over the meaning of that place in the community as well as the identities of those who sought to occupy that space.[3]

The large stone facade of Little Rock's Central High School is still imposing. Standing more than six stories high and spanning two city blocks, Central became the locus of a civil rights battle that would awaken viewers to the depths of Southern racism and White terror. Although African American adults in the community seemed less than surprised at the virulence of the White response—adjourning schools in the community early on the day the *Brown* decision was handed down for fear of white reprisals—few others seemed to have anticipated the eruption of White hostility over the legal mandate to desegregate.[4] Perhaps because other Arkansas school districts had accomplished integration with few instances of violence, or because Little Rock was believed to be one of the more moderate communities in Arkansas around issues of race, the scenes that unfolded around the implementation of integration were truly spectacular (Kirk, *Beyond Little Rock*, 5). Legal challenges to the gradual desegregation plan drawn up by the Little Rock superintendent of schools, Virgil T. Blossom, were filed by the Capital Citizens' Council in Little Rock; a White segregationist parents' group, the Mothers' League of Central High, requested delays in implementing the plan; and enraged White crowds gathered by the hundreds, sometimes as many as a thousand by some estimates,[5] throughout September 1957 to protest the admission of the African American teenagers to Central (Kirk, *Beyond Little Rock*, 109). *Warriors Don't Cry: A Searing Memoir of the Battle to Integrate Little Rock's Central High*, written by Melba Pattillo Beals, chronicles the terrible and traumatic 1957 school year when she and eight others idealistically volunteered to be the first African Americans to integrate Central. They had all fantasized about how wonderful it would be to attend the school, but in their youthful excitement they had not anticipated the kind of virulent and sustained resistance they would face on nearly all fronts, from adults and students alike. Before the students were able to successfully walk into the school building under federal protection, the battle was squarely waged outside, where White mobs tried to prevent the Nine from entering. Within the school, however, the situation was just as volatile. Strategies to derail integration in that space focused on harassment and violence. The goal was to incite a response from the Nine that would get them expelled, or to intimidate them into "voluntarily" leaving. Beals writes that during that year she was constantly terrified, wondering, "What will they do to me today? Will I make it to my homeroom? Who will be the first to slap me, to kick me in the shin, or call me nigger?" (xxiii). These were more than simply rhetorical questions for Beals; these fearful musings were her attempt to make sense of a familiar yet unfathomable Whiteness that threatened her every day of that long school year.

It is Beals's attempt to make sense of the alien and unknown that marks *Warriors Don't Cry* as part of the literature of white estrangement. What the youthful narrator seeks to understand in the dislocated time and space of the memoir is the connection between what she experiences of White identity in the school and the broader community of her youth and the place that enables these regressive and oppressive subjectivities to be forged with so little challenge or resistance within Whiteness. As Beals recognizes, Central High is the space in which a new Black identity is forged for the Little Rock Nine—they become warriors—but it is also the place where Whiteness is constructed in response to challenges from a variety of locations: federal legal statutes, local politicians and elected officials, grassroots organizations, and a generational attitudinal shift among

African Americans throughout the country. Both blacks and whites are shaped by their presence and interactions in this contested space, but her narrative specifically encourages us to consider how fictive kin groups are imagined and created through space and place and how violence was used to buttress and solidify those ties within Whiteness. Moreover, writings like Beals's memoir challenge us to recognize not simply that Whiteness uses space to defend preconceived notions of White racial identity, but rather that place shapes, and perhaps even constitutes at a very fundamental level, subjectivity. In the South of the 1950s and 1960s, the organization and segregation of space was an inextricable part of how Whiteness understood itself, so much so that transgressions into spaces that were once marked as "White" were experienced by whites as a disintegration of their very identity. White violence in the context of desegregation, then, was not simply Whiteness defending its spatial privilege. Rather, my readings suggest that this violence was a psychological defense against and sociological response to a fundamental challenge to the White self.

It has only been within the past ten to fifteen years, since the turn of the twenty-first century, that scholars in the field of geography have come to embrace the insights of cultural studies and critical race studies to reframe the ways in which their field conceptualizes and theorizes the connection between "race" and space/place. Prior to the 1970s, most of the conversation around race within geography centered on mapping distributions of racialized bodies within geographic areas. According to Alastair Bonnett, during this period geography was problematically intertwined with various imperial projects, and, ultimately, these early approaches to considering race provided justification for the domination of certain groups of people. By the 1970s, however, these methods were regularly critiqued by geographers and, according to Bonnett, there was more willingness in the field to "relate geography to social theory" (869). The result of this shift was that geographers began to analyze the social, cultural, and economic interactions of different "races" or ethnic groups to consider the quality and quantity of exchanges among differentiated groups within a particular geographic area. Yet this work did not include analyses of Whiteness as a racial category, leaving the focus on people of color as the only groups to which discussions of "race" could apply. This focus also presumed that race was stable and transparent and did not consider the "production and management of 'racial' meaning" as part of its project (Bonnett, 870).

More recently, the field of geography has embraced social constructivism as the dominant theoretical and ideological basis by which race is examined. As Tim Cresswell articulates in *Place: A Short Introduction*, "geographers informed by Marxism, feminism, and post-structuralism" focus on "how places are socially constructed and how these constructions are founded on acts of exclusion" (26). These approaches, as well as those more aptly classified as cultural geography, see "race" as always in the process of being created and assert that those constructions of race and place are expressions of particular ideologies and acts of power. In other words, they recognize that space/place is a primary way in which racial meaning is produced, and that power is the means by which those associations and spaces are assigned. In fact, the field now seems on the verge of embracing the idea that identity is formed in tandem with place rather than place being shaped after (racial) identity is formed, and while ultimately this may be a chicken-or-egg question of firsts, the assertion that place and identity are mutually constitutive seems to be substantiated by Beals's memoir.

Concurrent with these developments in geography studies, critical interest in White violence exploded with the emergence of critical whiteness studies as an academic field. Approaches to the study of this violence are as varied as the disciplines that engage the topic and as idiosyncratic as the scholars who conduct the research,[6] but they all move forward our understanding of racial violence by offering us new, more nuanced ways of thinking about, and vocabulary for analyzing, phenomenon that we thought we already understood. The growing complexity of the picture we have of lynching, race riots, or sundown towns, for instance, is due in large part to the willingness of scholars to continue probing and questioning knowledge we had come to take as definitive rather than contingent. What these approaches do not do so well, however, is examine White violence as a generality with specific expression, as an expression of power that has had various faces over time but that has consistently been exerted on Black bodies. This is the argument that Herbert Shapiro makes in *White Violence and Black Response: From Reconstruction to Montgomery*, as he seeks to bring the "scope and character" of white racism and violence into critical consciousness and discourse (xvi). By doing so, he calls attention to the fact that "Americans have been conditioned to associate violence with the behavior of black people," completely eliding the historical reality of White racist violence "employed to preserve outmoded social, political, and economic institutions" (xi–xii). James Clarke highlights the same in *The Lineaments of Wrath: Race, Violent Crime, and American Culture,* when he concludes from his longitudinal study of the black underclass that there is an "enduring pattern of violence that has defined relations between whites and blacks," a pattern in which African Americans "lived with a continuing threat of arbitrary acts of white brutality for which there was virtually no recourse" (xiv). Debra Walker King, author of *African Americans and the Culture of Pain,* states the case most concisely when she says that her book considers black pain (both as a material reality as well as a metaphor, I would argue) "as a persistent and essential strategy of Anglo American nation building and power exchange . . . a hidden persuasion of U.S. socialization" (21). These three scholars, like the literature of white estrangement in general, acknowledge that the one constant of White violence is that people of color broadly, and African American people in particular, have suffered immeasurable physical and psychological harm at the hands of people who thought of themselves as, or who wanted to be accepted as, White.

Warriors Don't Cry provides an exemplary opportunity for considering the complicated interconnection between White (group) identity and violence, an analysis that has been, with few exceptions, consistently deferred in dominant critical and social analyses. As part of the literature of white estrangement, however, *Warriors* joins a long history of representation and analysis of whiteness as "terrible . . . terrifying . . . [and] terrorizing" (hooks, "Representations of Whiteness," 170). Whether emerging from the period of slavery, the Reconstruction and Harlem Renaissance eras, or the decades of the Civil Rights movement,[7] the literature of white estrangement presents and represents White violence as anything but an anomaly. Often arbitrary, unreasoned, and gratuitous, this violence is rampant, waged to inspire terror and to satisfy a bloodthirst that at times seems unquenchable. The sociological, critical, and literary engagements with White violence within the literature of white estrangement call attention to it as a salient feature of Whiteness and analyze it as a long-standing (and continuing) social problem for the body politic of America. It is a particular analysis of Whiteness that calls for fuller attention because, if taken seriously and in its totality, it suggests the need to radically reframe our understanding of Whiteness by deeply engaging the persistent reality of White violence.

In his essay "Racial Exploitation and the Wages of Whiteness," philosopher Charles W. Mills anticipates the point I want to make here.

Mills argues that the conceptualization of the United States "as basically an egalitarian (if a bit flawed) liberal democracy free of the hierarchical structures of the Old World" is fundamentally misguided (27). Rather, he asserts, we need a new paradigm that will allow us to recognize the "basic structure" of the U.S. political and social systems as "unjust," and to begin, thereby, to consider other possibilities for social organization (29). Likewise, I believe that the prevailing narrative of Whiteness as either meaningless (as in, without meaning or significance in the world) or a benign element of White racial subjectivity, is a gross misreading of the historical record. Whiteness has not been kind. Its first impulse has not been toward inclusion and egalitarianism. Instead, as James Baldwin argues, Whiteness has an "appallingly oppressive and bloody history known all over the world," and as more of the history of white violence and brutality is recovered—from the forced relocation and holocaust of Native Americans to Japanese internment, from whippings and brandings to dismemberment and lynching, from medical experimentation to Jim Crow, and from Chinese and Latino labor exploitation to the intentional creation of all-white communities in modern-day America—there is increasing reason to consider White racial supremacy, injustice, and violence as the bedrock of White social and political identity ("Guilt," 409). My attempt to bring analyses of space/place to bear on the subjects of White identity and violence is an effort to challenge the continued framing of White terror—both outside the academy as well as within it—as sporadic or episodic. Instead, I posit a framework in which we can begin to recognize White violence as the recurring, persistent, national, and international foundation of White subjectivity that it in fact has been.

This chapter considers the insights and contributions of Melba Pattillo Beals as well as other African American artists and intellectuals of the Civil Rights era who struggled not only to document White violence but also to highlight the multiple levels at which it worked to support and reinforce white identity and sociology in the United States. Beals's recounting of the brutal year she spent integrating Central High adds to existing historical analyses of White violence by introducing a postmodern understanding of identity to the discourse. The key to surviving her year at Central High School when she was a teen, and to crafting a revealing and compelling memoir as an adult, is rooted in her ability to understand how White identity was forged through particular uses of space, place, and violence, the ways in which violence and space interacted to *produce* Whiteness in a specific context.

In 1957, Central High School was thirty years old and provided one hundred classrooms for more than eighteen hundred white students from Little Rock and surrounding communities. Built at a cost of $1.5 million, it was the most expensive school building in the United States at that time, and it was recognized by the National Institute of Architects as "America's Most Beautiful High School." It was faced in brick, featured colonnades of cut stone, and sported soaring windows, massive wooden doors, and decorative arches and sculpture. Inside, ceramic corridors and wooden floors were laid throughout (Freeman). It was well maintained and well resourced, and White students attending the school had solid opportunities to later attend the best colleges and universities in the nation.

For African Americans, the school had traditionally represented all of the opportunities that would forever be out of their reach. This message, reinforced by decades of custom and policy and maintained by the threat and history of White violence, was so deeply ingrained in much of Little Rock's Black community that some did not support actions that would disrupt the racial contract[8] under which Blacks and Whites interacted. Yet the expansiveness of Central High's structure was a constant reminder of all that the Black community did not have, and the school's limited accessibility—prohibited to all African Americans except those employed in the school—made it a source of curiosity, envy, and wonder. To the seventy African American students who indicated an interest in attending and the nine who remained after Superintendent Blossom implemented a contested "screening process" to handpick those who would be admitted, Central offered the promise of superior educational facilities, a wider range of classes, and improved prospects and preparation for college (Kirk, *Redefining*, 107). It also symbolized a radical change in the legal and, potentially, social status of African Americans. To attend Central meant that one was at the forefront of history, opening doors that had long been barred to one's family and community. The young Beals reasoned, "if schools were open to my people, I would also get access to other opportunities I had been denied" (28). Carlotta Walls Lanier, another of the Little Rock Nine, writes of the approach that brought the students to the door of Central: "In tandem, we began to move slowly, deliberately— off the curb, up the walkway, past the fountain, up the left set of steps, and then up the next set. Finally, I stood at that grand entrance with its heavy wooden doors, surrounded by so much brick and stone" (98). Clearly at this moment the door, a synecdoche for Central High itself, signifies everything that had been denied to Lanier and her peers. The prospect not only of getting into the school but of entering through the front door and all that that entrance symbolized is foregrounded in this moment. Central was the portal through which a newly freed, fully recognized African American citizen would emerge; it represented the promise and reality of change for African Americans. Ironically, however, the solidity and impressiveness of the entryway that so awes Lanier was created by the very same materials—brick, stone, and heavy wood—that had previously communicated the permanent exclusion of African Americans from all that lay within. Nothing but the sociospatial meaning of the place had shifted; it was *their* relationship to the building that had changed.

Similarly, although Central High had always been a segregated space, the significance of the school among Whites in and around Little Rock, what we might call Central High as a *place*, was also in flux. For many whites, the school stood for the cherished traditions and racial norms of the South. Its massive presence and well-maintained landscape reminded all of the benefits of White privilege and the meaningful payoffs to those who invested in Whiteness. However, Central High was slated as the only White high school to be desegregated as part of the "Blossom plan," a blueprint for gradual integration in the Little Rock School District; two new schools were also proposed under the plan, one in the "predominantly black eastern part of the city" and the other, Hall High, in the "affluent white western suburbs" of Little Rock (Kirk, *Redefining*, 94). Although assurances were made that both of the new schools would be integrated, John Kirk argues that the new sites were attempts to minimally comply with, and ultimately subvert, *Brown*, efforts that were strengthened after the Supreme Court failed in the *Brown II* decision to establish a definitive timeline by which desegregation had to occur. In fact, in the wake of *Brown II*, the Blossom plan was modified in such a way that elite white students residing in the suburbs were allowed to transfer, if they chose, to Hall High. Students of color as well as middle- and working-class whites in the community were prohibited from doing the same even if they lived in closer proximity to Hall than to other schools. Believing that Whiteness and the "Southern way of life" were under siege and desiring nothing so much as that things would remain unchanged in their lives,[9] the "middle strata" of Southern whites soon recognized that upper-class whites were being sheltered from the requirements of the new law. The significant social and psychological work of desegregation was being required of whites differently according to their socioeconomic status. Central High School became a wellspring of white class antagonism as working-class whites began to sense this even greater betrayal that situated them as the victims of a class-based, *intra*-racial violence.

Historian after historian has pointed to how unprepared White Southerners were for the Civil Rights movement, how invested they were in the belief that race relations in their communities were "good," especially if there previously had been an "absence of trouble and submissive acceptance [of racial stratification] on the part of Negroes" in their communities (Sokol, 59). In the face of these fantasies of racial harmony, they were completely unable to anticipate the reality of an unarticulated dissatisfaction and discontent among African Americans. When civil rights agitation did arrive, Whites were often outraged as well as shocked, fueling a range of responses that were fevered but that did not often produce significant changes in attitudes or allegiances. Similarly, the dawning understanding that Little Rock's whites were not to be equally subject to desegregation legislation and that, in fact, the Whiteness of some was deemed more worthy of protection than that of others, must have been disappointing, if not surprising, for many of the city's middle- and working-class whites.[10] Yet their sense of betrayal would not have been enough to dislodge their commitment to Whiteness. Given the complexity of forces and circumstances that whites were essentially responding to in Little Rock, it seems reasonable to question the received narrative that White resistance was only a response to the imminent entry of nine African American students to Central High. It is just as likely that their virulent demonstrations can fruitfully be understood as an attempt to reclaim a privileged racial identity that they believed was being compromised by the maneuvers of elite whites in Little Rock. Opposing desegregation was a way of reasserting a connection with and an allegiance to a Whiteness that had become more obviously fragmented and disparate in the wake of *Brown*. Thus, the desegregation battle that became so prominent across the color line was first a battle *within* Whiteness, an attempt by Little Rock's middle- and working-class whites to reclaim the defining privileges of Whiteness at the very moment that they were seemingly being expulsed from the social body of Whiteness.

Geographer Edward Relph writes in *Place and Placelessness* that "identity is a basic feature of our experience of places which both influences and is influenced by those experiences . . . it is not just the identity *of* a place that is important, but also the identity that a person or group has *with* that place" (45). Similarly, in "Creating Geographies of Difference," David Sibley asserts, "We can usefully assume that the values of residents and the values expressed in the material environment are mutually rein-forcing" (118). What both of these scholars point to is the inextricability of place and human identity, the fact that our building and organization of space both reflects and constitutes who we are, a recursive interactivity that Edward Soja refers to as a "socio-spatial dialectic" (57). The choice to design a community around a town square with all public walks and streets emanating from it, for instance, clearly privileges community life and interaction; the design communicates a set of values. Once materially in the world, however, that design also makes inhabitants more likely to value those things themselves, as the "structure" of the place enables more interactions and encourages connection among people who might oth-erwise pursue individualism and anonymity within the community. Even further, our identities are shaped by the interactions we have within that artificially constructed space. The town center, with its increased oppor-tunities for interaction and exchange, becomes important to us as a place not only for what the space represents in the abstract, but also because of what happens in that place of increased communal exchange.

The same dialectics of place and identity existed for working-class and segregationist whites in Little Rock and much of the South. Segregated spaces were integral to White identity. They were not only bound up in the experience of certain places being cordoned off, reserves of Whiteness, but also inextricably linked to a sense of White superiority in the region. First, racially exclusive spaces evidenced the power of Whiteness to shape the world in ways that benefited itself. Blackness was made not to matter in the material allocations of the larger social structure, which was also reflected in the spaces and services made available to African Americans. Segregated spaces, then, evidenced the social investment in the superior-ity of Whiteness, because these white racial preserves were often much better maintained and equipped than similarly purposed spaces desig-nated as "black." Additionally, it was important to and for Whiteness that the choice of how and when to segregate was only available to the group in power; Whites had full access to and movement in all spaces, both "white" and "black," while the same freedom of movement was denied to African Americans. This made access to space and freedom of movement integral components of White subjectivities, two of the means by which White-ness understood itself as distinct from, and more privileged than, Black-ness. Finally, social segregation enabled a certain ego-stroking sense of the White self to emerge and be reinforced. Spatial segregation, as Malcolm X insightfully points out, never truly existed.[11] Segregated spaces were never fully White; Black bodies were always present in menial, subservient positions. As such, Whites were most often interacting with African Americans who were forced to perform deference and inferiority in these spaces, no matter what their accomplishment. By controlling the types of exchanges that were likely to occur across the color line in the interracial contact zone of the South, Whites were able to maintain and believe the illusion that Whiteness was exceptional and superior. For all of these reasons, agitation that sought to dismantle this spatial caste system was particularly threatening for Southern Whites. Segregated space not only was shaped by those who understood themselves as White, but also helped to shape White subjectivities in profound ways.

The equating of well-maintained, segregated spaces with a social and racial hierarchy that elevated Whiteness was the social psychology that Mamie and Kenneth Clark tapped into with their doll experiments in the 1930s, the results of which were so important to the desegregation lawsuits of the fifties. Mamie Clark began the exploration of racial identification and self-awareness in children as research for her master's thesis in 1939. She and her husband, Kenneth, refined that research and developed the Dolls Test as collaborators, coauthoring several reports of their findings. The test was administered to two groups of African American children: a Southern group who attended segregated nursery schools and a Northern group who attended integrated schools. Students in both groups "preferred the white doll and attributed positive characteristics to it." Both groups also devalued their own racial identities, although children from the North tended to become upset when asked to say which doll looked most like them, while children from the South "accommodated more to their negative racial identity." The Clarks concluded that "prejudice, discrimination *and segregation*" caused self-hatred in African American children in their formative years (quoted in Gibbons and Van Nort, 30; emphasis mine). African Americans and whites alike who were raised in the South, where these spatialized messages about the relative value of the races were ubiquitous, internalized the social investment in White superiority and supremacy. Many African Americans, however, retained the capacity to imagine alternative geographies and to embrace a vision of a more open and just society despite their socialization, a resistant framing of geographical connection and belonging that Tim Cresswell refers to as "heretical geography."[12] However, according to Kenneth Clark, challenges to the racial and spatial status quo activated particular anxieties and even crises within Whiteness. As he writes, in the absence of racial prejudice and social mores that maintained the appearance of Black inferiority, Whites would have to face the "devastating realization of . . . [their] own social, economic, sexual, or intellectual inadequacies" (75). Thus, decisions to desegregate Central High and other social institutions and spaces called into question the meaning of Whiteness *for Whites* in profound ways, largely by transforming the identity that was possible within those places for White Americans.

Like the adult Beals who opens *Warriors Don't Cry* with a powerful sense of dislocation and confusion, traditional Southern White identity was in a state of disintegration as a result of efforts toward social and spatial integration in the South. This disintegration of social and personal identity fueled white paranoia and made their rhetoric and actions even more illogical and dangerous. Facing the reality of new laws, divergent class interests, and a new generation of African American activists, and with "no preparation in mind or heart or culture for relating to Negroes outside of the segregated pattern," the average Southern White began to equate the desegregation of spaces with other interpersonal interactions and exchanges, like dating and marriage (Thurman, 11). The words uttered by a White woman as she assaulted the teenaged Melba are revealing:

> Suddenly I felt it—the sting of a hand slapping the side of my cheek, and then warm slimy saliva on my face . . .
> A woman stood toe-to-toe with me, not moving. "Nigger!" she shouted in my face again and again . . . Her face was distorted by rage. "Nigger bitch. Why don't you go home?" she lashed out at me. "Next thing, you'll want to marry one of our children." (Beals, 111)

Aside from the violence of encounters like this, which I will discuss in more detail shortly, what is noteworthy here is the progression of thought evidenced in the words of the attacker: from spatial integration to marriage. This was a logic that seemed natural, almost inevitable, for many White Southerners. However, the anxiety voiced in exchanges like this, which were repeated so often in the fifties and sixties as to have constituted a mantra of White segregationists and "average" white Americans alike, was far more than the mythic Southern concern over the threat of "amalgamation." Rather, in unguarded verbal explosions like this we see most clearly the significance of space to Southern White identity, for this outburst really only seems logical if one understands a metonymic relationship between Whiteness and segregated space: "White places" (i.e., segregated spaces) have become interchangeable with the White body. To enter one protected space, according to this logic, was to penetrate the other. Here we approach the central reason African Americans so often stood accused of desiring the White body when they walked through a door as social equals. The anxiety surrounding desegregation for many White Americans was the result of a spatial understanding of the White self.

In "A Phenomenology of Whiteness," philosopher Sara Ahmed argues that a key to understanding Whiteness lies in our attentiveness to the ways in which bodies, and by extension identities, are established and oriented in space. She writes of the "body-at-home" that "extends into space through how it reaches towards objects that are already 'in place.'" This body is one that does not experience friction or resistance in or from its surroundings, "does not pose 'a problem' or an obstacle to the action." Rather, the body-at-home, or "habitual body," is one that "goes unnoticed" because the body *"does not command attention"* in its movements in and through its environment (153, 156). Its environment is comfortable, an easy fit, allowing the body to extend its reach almost effortlessly in space. These arrangements, according to Ahmed, often constitute a "spatial form of inheritance" where "spaces also take shape by being oriented around some bodies, more than others" (157). In a White supremacist culture, space is an extension of the white body because, unlike bodies of color, the white body-at-home (the white self) does not call attention to itself as it performs, nor does it experience its Whiteness as an obstacle to action. In this way, Whiteness experiences most spaces as extensions of the white body.

The *Brown v. Board of Education* decision, however, immediately made Whiteness visible and contested, both within Whiteness as well as externally. The nine brown bodies that were set to enter Central High disrupted the seamless extension of the White body-at-home. Where once the race of the body-at-home held no meaning, now the White body was "'stressed' in [its] encounters with objects or others" as it became an object of scrutiny and reflection (Ahmed, 156). The need to think about one's Whiteness was established no matter what one's political or ideological beliefs, and that need for self-awareness and self-reflection unmasked the diversity of "white" identities, experiences, and interests within the community. This unmasking, in turn, fundamentally challenged the social codes and silences that created a normative, if not monolithic, Whiteness. Additionally, while the Supreme Court decision did not immediately make Whiteness an obstacle to action, the concomitant decision to enforce the ruling with military power did seek to limit a certain performance of Whiteness that directly challenged federal legislation and power. In this way, Whiteness became something that was limited in its reach. The place that had once invited and allowed the easy extension of the White self was now legally redefined as a space that would accommodate people who could, through their presence as social equals, transform the meaning of the place for Whites and Blacks alike. Thus, integration created a fissure in the facade of Whiteness, and the school as well as other spaces that were being desegregated became places where Whiteness was a subject of attention rather than an un(re)marked orientation.[13] In ways that had never been widely possible before, integration forced a recognition that the white body (as well as the body of Whiteness) was both "raced" and "classed."

Beals extends the logic of White spatialized bodies to great effect in her memoir in moments when she begins to consider what the interior spaces of Central High suggest about the interiority, or psychology, of Whiteness. The "gigantic brick building that looked so much like a big Eastern university," she tells us, was surrounded by "manicured lawns and trees, with a pond in front," with the "kind of look . . . that tells you folks have budgeted lots of money to keep things nice" (42–43). However, Beals soon realizes, "the reality was so much bigger, darker, and more treacherous" (110). That well-maintained exterior concealed a "twisted maze of . . . hallway[s]," spiral staircases, dimly lit rooms and alcoves, and isolated entrances where "no teacher, principles, or guards" kept watch, interior spaces that she juxtaposes to the well-ordered, beautiful exterior (113, 248). The sum of her descriptions encourages us to read these interior, labyrinthine spaces as a metaphor for the troubled complexities of a collective White consciousness. The structure is domineering, meant to inspire awe, but is also impossible to navigate, with many spaces where one is able to hide from view of others as well as one's self. Beals's invitation to interrogate the interior spaces of Central High as an externalization of the White psyche is perhaps most evident when she encourages readers to consider the reason for the extreme resistance she and others face as they pursue integration. She writes, "I sometimes wish I could change myself into a psychiatrist to determine what makes me such a hated member of this school. Can they really be treating me this way simply because I am brown, that's all" (241). Of note here is Beals's assertion that the proper discipline for demystifying White resistance and violence is not sociology, economics, or history, but psychiatry.

Warriors Don't Cry also makes it clear that there is little positive growth happening for most Whites in Central High, academically, socially, or emotionally. Beals notes a number of classes in which teachers seem to have abdicated control of their classrooms to segregationist students, refusing to see or respond to the harassment that the Nine experienced. These educators implicitly say, as one of their colleagues did outright when asked to "calm people down" in her class, "'I hope you don't think we're gonna browbeat our students to please you'all'" (136). In other moments, Beals acknowledges that moderate White students were pressured to ostracize African American students and that "the principal, vice-principals, and teachers had lost any hopes of corralling belligerent students . . . hooligans [who] completely ignor[ed] commands to cease their outrageous behavior" (300). The picture that emerges is of a Whiteness with no internal or external controls, one that allows its fear and resentment to escalate to paranoia over "rumors" that African Americans wanted to "rule" over Whites (180). By the end of the school year, Melba notes, "The hallways were like a three-ring circus . . . there were no longer islands of sanity within the insanity of that school" (300). If, as Ahmed argues, "spaces acquire the shape of the bodies that 'inhabit' them," Central now mirrors the madness of the broader White response to desegregation (156). It is not only an extension of the (White) body, as segregationists perhaps want it to be read, but also indicative of the White mind.

In light of the suggestive ways that Beals's narrative yokes issues of conflicted White identities with the modalities of segregated space and contested place, a comment made by then-governor Faubus, from which I draw the title of this chapter, takes on new registers of meaning. He lamented, as recorded by Beals, "We are now an occupied territory" (128). While his comment clearly was meant to reference the arrival of federal troops in Little Rock to ensure that nine African American teens would be able to attend Central High in compliance with federal law, the words also allow us to witness Whiteness "undressed and from the back and side," to borrow Du Bois's words, revealing more of itself than it would consciously disclose ("White Folk," 923). For Whiteness did become an "occupied territory" on several different levels in this era: in the ways that space suddenly became a site of contested power, requiring Whites to fight to retain certain spatial privileges that had once been so widely defended and infrequently challenged as to seem natural; in the ways that Southern Whites, in particular, became preoccupied with crafting a response to a sociocultural revolution that would challenge the structures of power and privilege in the United States; and in the imperative that whites confront their own heterogeneity and the myriad, sometimes conflicting position-alities that that diversity implied. Whiteness was also "occupied," though, in the sense that the presence of resistant African American subjects in places that had been preserved as protected spaces of Whiteness necessi-tated that Whites make meaning of that African American presence, both in terms of how to understand that defiant subject as well as how to think about racial Whiteness in this changing social context.

Of course, it does not necessarily follow that the heightened aware-ness of Whiteness as a raced and classed subjectivity with socially legitimated power (as opposed to "natural" superiority) will lead to a reenvisioning of the possibilities of Whiteness by those who so identify. In fact, as I have argued elsewhere in this book, sociocultural challenges to Whiteness historically have led to a rearticulation that has simply sought to justify Whiteness on a different front. Often, as was the case at Central High, the reassertion of the power and privilege of Whiteness is enacted through racial terror. *Warriors Don't Cry* certainly articulates this potentiality when Beals records the pervasive fear of Whiteness evi-dent among the adults in her home and community. She testifies to the verbal affronts her mother had to endure from white insurance collec-tors who visited their home, her grandmother's sweaty palms when they were interrogated by white police officers after Beals went to the whites-only bathroom in a department store, and her father's suppressed rage as he was encouraged to passively witness his family's violations to ensure his own survival. The young Beals also registers the "stiffening" of her mother's body and the "fear in her eyes" when they had to run errands in Little Rock's "uptown" (7). "By the time I was three years old," she writes, "I was already . . . afraid of white people. . . . My folks never explained that I should be frightened of those white people. My fear developed as I observed adults and listened to their conversations" (6). Blacks lived in a climate of fear, their psyches, and often even their bodies, bracing for the demeaning word, the degradation, the social injury, or the violent blow at the hands of a random white person.

These large and small aggressions, threats, and acts of terror were of little consequence to White people, however. They were part of the machin-ery of Whiteness and, if anything, were the source of honor and respect within White communities. Indeed, John Hope Franklin argues that in the South in particular violence had been "institutionalized" and had had "bestowed on it an aura of respectability" that made it a marker of status rather than a source of shame (ix). This tacit acceptance of White violence lasted well into the mid-twentieth century and did not significantly abate until White terror was nationally televised and reported during the 1950s and 1960s. The aggression and violence faced by African American citizen-activists of those decades were so extreme that white Americans outside the South could no longer deny it, or sanction it, as an alter ego of Whiteness. Racism and the violence it often gave birth to was a spirit that knew no bounds; whites as well as blacks could and did fall victim, a fact that the Student Nonviolent Coordinating Committee (SNCC) leadership exploited in its decision to bring "an army of Northern college students" to the Southern campaign for social justice. As SNCC staffer and organizer John Lewis explains in his memoir of the movement, *Walking with the Wind*, "Our people were essentially being slaughtered down there. If white America would not respond to the deaths of our people, the thinking went, maybe it would react to the deaths of its *own* children" (250). Images of bombed churches and buses; bloated, disfigured, and discarded bodies recovered from wooded areas, streams, creeks, and swamps; fire hoses and attack dogs turned against nonviolent protesters, all attest to the enormity of the threat that faced those who dared to work toward the dream of a democratic society. In Mississippi alone during a three-month period in 1964, civil rights workers reported to the SNCC's central headquarters more than 450 attacks, which included eighty beatings, thirty-five shootings, thirty-five church burnings, and thirty bombings (John Lewis, 274). Those who survived still seem stunned, shell-shocked, even decades later, by their experiences. Many did not survive. The banality of this evil exploded into the national consciousness in the mid-1960s as national media coverage made racism and White terror in the region impossible to deny. Slowly, America's complacency dissipated; fewer and fewer people were willing to tacitly accept White violence. A decade earlier, however, when Beals and eight other children were admitted to Little Rock Central High, America's moral censorship of White racist violence had not yet solidified. The Little Rock Nine, like the whole of the black community, lived with the knowledge that they could become victims at any time, in any context, and for any reason.

Nowhere is that reality more apparent than in the attack the youthful Beals suffered on the day that the *Brown* decision was handed down. In recognition of the reprisals that might follow the ruling, schools serving African American students in Little Rock were dismissed early, and twelve-year-old Beals walked home, unescorted, as she had done since she was six. As she crossed a field, she was confronted by a "big white man . . . broad and huge, like a wrestler," offering her candy and a ride in his car (25). Frightened by his size and the tone of his unfamiliar voice, she fled and was pursued by him. Her account details his rage and the "reason" for his attack:

> I couldn't hear anything except for the sound of my saddle shoes pounding the ground and the thud of his feet close behind me. That's when he started talking about "niggers" wanting to go to school with his children and how he wasn't going to stand for it. . . . I felt his strong hands clutch my back. . . . He pulled me down and turned me on my back. . . . He slapped me hard across the face. I covered my eyes with my hands and waited for him to strike me again. Instead, I felt him squirm against me, and then I saw him taking his pants down. . . . His huge fist smashed hard against my face. . . .
>
> "I'll show you niggers the Supreme Court can't run my life," he said as his hand ripped at my underpants. A voice inside my head told me I was going to die, that there was nothing I could do about it. White men were in charge. (25–26)

Although the attack is disrupted and Beals is able to escape her would-be rapist, this horrific violence leaves the child physically and psychologically battered. She feels ashamed that she has been touched by a "strange man," and her family makes the decision not to report the attack because "white police are liable to do something worse to her than what already happened." Instead, her grandmother instructs her to "pray for that evil white man, pray every day for twenty-one days, asking God to forgive him and teach him right" (27). This guidance, although counterintuitive, has the desired effect. It impresses upon Beals that the white man who attacked her was the one who should feel shame for his actions, and it teaches her that she can question, and even condemn, White hatred and fear without becoming hateful and fearful herself. At the end of the twenty-one days of prayer, she writes, "I have to keep up with what the men on the Supreme Court are doing. That way I can stay home on the day the justices vote decisions that make white men want to rape me" (28). Here we see Beals beginning to probe the White psyche, beginning to seek understanding that will help her anticipate the catalysts to White rage and violence. She has moved from passively accepting that "white men were in charge" to a spirit of interrogation and analysis, a stance that subverts at least some of the power of Whiteness.

As readers, we are initiated on a similar journey by the extreme utterances of the attacker. We hear the announcement that he intends to prove that the Supreme Court "can't run" his life, and we witness his anger over the circumscription of White power set in motion by the Court's decision. Yet his unreasoned act is completely unresponsive to the source of his frustration and fear, and instead reveals how fragile his sense of empowered White selfhood really is. Patricia Hill Collins and others have pointed out that the black woman's body, through stereotypes and mythologies of the Mammy, has been constructed by mainstream media and discourse as nurturing, comforting, and servile.[14] As a not-yet-matured female body, however, the young Beals represents a generation who has implicitly rejected White control over their bodies and images. Her presence, even when moving within a black community, is an implicit threat to Whiteness. Thus, for her assailant, raping this youthful body, which had become a powerful symbol of self-possession and imminent social change, would enable him to reassert his power and control as a White man. Ironically, however, his irrational act does just the opposite. Readers are instead made acutely aware of the attacker's power*less*ness, for only desperation would allow him to believe that violating a child's body would stabilize his sense of himself as a dominant, masterful White male.

While Beals certainly details the physical acts of violence that she experiences as a youthful crusader for access and equality, more generally her memoir chronicles the violence that is inherent in social policies that separate people based, in this case, on race. Segregation is, in and of itself, a form of spatialized violence. It is an "attack . . . on the dignity and integrity" of those who are denied equal access to the spaces and places used by other people (Thurman, 5). It also gives rise to different, more explicitly physical acts of violence, as those in power seek to establish and/ or retain their spatial privilege and exclusionary practices. An example of this truth of segregation can be found in the phenomenon of sundown towns, defined by James Loewen, author of *Sundown Towns: A Hidden Dimension of American Racism*, as "any organized jurisdiction that for decades kept African Americans or other groups from living in it" (4). While these white racial communities could be created through ordinance or threat of violence, sundown towns were often established through acts of White terror, like lynchings or White riots, in which homes, businesses, and community structures (churches, community centers, etc.) of the targeted group were destroyed. They are maintained through many of the same threats and accretions of history, and, over time, even residents who know the specific histories that created their communities begin to think of them as naturally and historically "all-white." Building on the nomenclature used to describe the systematic murder and expulsion of ethnic groups in central Europe, Elliot Jaspin, author of *Buried in the Bitter Waters*, refers to this obfuscated history of White America as "racial cleansings" to emphasize the deliberate, methodical elimination of African Americans from communities across the country (13).

While Arkansas's state capital, Little Rock, was clearly not a sundown town in 1957, like many cities and towns in the South and throughout the United States in the fifties and sixties, it was a harshly segregated space. The social separation of Whites and Blacks was maintained through custom, violence, and threat of harm. As discussed earlier in this chapter, Little Rock's segregated places had become bound up with White group identity; they instilled in Whites a sense of freedom and superiority while masking the diverse and often conflicting goals that existed within Whiteness. But in the face of legal redefinitions of institutional spaces that disrupted Whiteness's metonymic relationship with space, class divisions threatened to fracture a tenuous White racial alliance. What emerged as a practice and a strategy to address the anxieties of many White Southerners was the use of violence to reassert a set of shared values within Whiteness. In this context, violence not only sought to reestablish the historic relationship between Whiteness and space but also was used to unify whites who had only recently been forced to recognize the diverse interests and perspectives that were represented in their group. In other words, White racial violence did not exist solely (or perhaps even primarily) to defend the privileges and authority of Whiteness, as was often asserted by white assailants and those who sought to explain and justify White terror. *Warriors Don't Cry* encourages us to be attentive to the ways that violence can be used to reassert or even *reconstruct* a Whiteness that has been destabilized in particular historical moments and geographic spaces.

Composed over a period of twenty years, Beals's account of her experiences as one of the Little Rock Nine begins with her return to the site in 1987 as part of a commemoration and reunion of the students—now adults—who had integrated Central High. She recounts that she "began the first draft of this book when I was eighteen, but in the ensuing years, I could not face the ghosts that its pages called up" (xvii). Haunted by the danger, cruelty, and brutality she faced daily during that school year, when she returns to Central thirty years later she is immediately transported back to her fifteen-year-old self:

As teenagers trying to reach the front door, we were trapped between a rampaging mob, threatening to kill us to keep us out, and armed soldiers of the Arkansas National Guard dispatched by the governor to block our entry.

. . . all this pomp and circumstance and the presence of my eight colleagues does not numb the pain I feel at entering Central High School, a building I remember only as a hellish torture chamber. . . . We have both relished and dreaded this moment when we would again walk up these stairs. (xix–xxi)

Beals's introduction immediately immerses us not in the commemoration ceremony that has brought the Nine back to Central, but in the terror and violence that they faced thirty years earlier. In response to a question from local reporters covering the return of the Little Rock Nine, Beals responds that attending Central was like going "off to war. . . . It was like being a soldier on a battlefield." Another, unnamed veteran of the war says that it "is frightening" to be back at Central—not that it *was* frightening thirty years ago, but that it *is* frightening in the present time (xxi). As rapid time shifts continue to destabilize both the narrator and her introduction of *Warriors Don't Cry*, readers are transported back to 1957 with the narrator. The dislocation and disintegration of the adult author Beals allows readers to contemplate her identity as a teen, even as the now youthful narrator seeks to make sense of the Whites who surround and threaten her almost daily.

The year Beals and her peers spend integrating Central High was horrific by any standard. She and the others were constant targets of harassment, small and large attacks that kept the group on heightened alert and in fear. Terrence Roberts, another of the Nine, acknowledges his "gut-wrenching fear" that school year and reflects that their experiences were "imprinted indelibly upon each of our brains; we remember well the terror we felt in our bones" (117, 118). He spent much of his time, he writes, "getting myself to some place of relative safety, out of the line of fire" and "paying attention to the immediate surroundings, gauging the potential for violence, and staying far away from such areas as much as possible" (119). Lanier says of her experience, "it was more of an internal battle: How do I dodge the heel walker? How do I hold my books to avoid attack? How do I manage to get through the day without using my locker or going to the girls' bathroom? The strain of calculating my every move was consuming" (98). These are but a small indication of their torture. Beals and her peers were showered daily by hostile words and glares; threatened with lynching; spit upon repeatedly; slapped; attacked by elbows jabbed painfully into their ribs, backs, and arms; shoved down stairs; kicked, punched, and stepped on until they bled; scalded with hot water; assaulted with books; stabbed with pointed objects; showered by balls of paper that had been set afire; and, in Melba's case, sprayed in her eyes with acid. These attacks were not only physical but in many cases and just as importantly psychological, designed to humiliate and demoralize the Nine. The violence reinforced their status as outsiders, unwanted interlopers. They were made even more powerless by the injunctions against retaliation they received from both White school officials, who were concerned that their response might lead to an uncontrollable, embarrassing White riot within the school, and the local NAACP, which was concerned about their safety. Having received "no training . . . in self-defense or in the ways of nonviolent protest or passive resistance," the Nine developed what survival mechanisms they could "on the job," and, as Lanier notes, "in the hallways between classes" (99).

It is of no small importance that Lanier mentions that so much of her training for survival occurred in common spaces like hallways; it is a common refrain in the memoirs published by the Little Rock Nine. Many of their attacks did indeed happen in large, crowded gathering places like the auditorium, cafeteria, girls' locker room, or hallways that were populated with hundreds of potentially hostile students between classes. Other areas of frequent attacks were the open spaces in and around the school, like the school's entrance, where angry mobs gathered, and the sporting field, protected from White protesters in the community at large by only a fence. These spaces, while certainly ideal for unpredictable attacks from individuals wishing to remain anonymous in the crowd, also had another benefit for those who sought to reclaim Central High as a segregated sanctuary for Whiteness. Violence in these common areas implicitly made accomplices of the hundreds of others who happened to be present during the attacks. The fear and apathy that prevented moderate whites from intervening forged a fictive kin group between them and the more vocal, organized segregationists. Their silence and inaction did not render them neutral, but instead made them collaborators in and supporters of the Whiteness that was being forged through that violence. Those common spaces and group experiences, which could have been spaces of recognition and community, were instead transformed into the source of the most severe alienation and aggression that occurred that year in Central High. They were the places where terroristic Whiteness was asserted most effectively precisely because they were places where everyone learned what it meant to belong to the family of Whiteness.

Tim Cresswell states that "places are never complete, finished or bounded but are always becoming—in process" (*Place: Short Introduction*, 37). One can certainly see that theorem at work in battles to integrate spaces that had formerly excluded certain people. The character of Little Rock's Central High, for instance, was potentially radically transformed, first by the legal mandate to desegregate, then by the actual bodies that entered the space. So, too, is spatialized identity constantly in process. The presence of African Americans in the school created a different "embodied relationship" with that place for both white and black Americans (Cresswell, *Place: Short Introduction*, 37). Beals says that she became a warrior as a result of the year she spent integrating Central High. While she may have entered as an idealistic, hopeful teen, her experiences necessitated that she become someone new in order to survive, a warrior who could evaluate the constantly changing context of her environment. She had to become adept at gauging levels of danger and risk, making immediate decisions about courses of action that could minimize harm, and distinguishing friend from foe. Her vantage point as an outsider to Central, and to Whiteness more generally, allowed her to discern the confluences between White identity, segregated space, and violence more clearly, and to make a decision about how she wanted to perform Blackness in response to those realities. Beals chose to be steadfast, determined, focused, and committed to her course of action, no matter how difficult the path. It was a decision that she did not, or perhaps could not, make until in that space, in that situation. Her understanding of her blackness, and the ways that she performed and navigated that racial identity in the world, both were shaped by her experiences in the school. Her identity as a warrior was forged in Central High.

Similarly, as Beals's narrative makes clear, Whiteness was being created in the space and context of the battle to desegregate Central High. Segregationist parents and students may have thought that they were defending the racial exclusivity of that space, but their actions actually *constructed* Whiteness in a particular way; they made a choice in that moment about how to be white, rather than asserting a stable, preexisting identity through their actions. Beals notes on several occasions that some of her White peers smiled at her or made other attempts to reach out to her in the beginning, but that they were "pressured to turn away" by being harassed, intimidated, and ostracized by other Whites (190). Roberts also mentions that "White students who befriended any of the nine of us were labeled 'nigger lovers' and harassed by those who wanted to preserve the old social order" (121). These moments of outreach were different articula-tions and understandings of Whiteness and represented the possibility for different performances of Whiteness to emerge. These moderate whites were attacked as viciously as the Nine, anticipating the observation of the theologian Thandeka that white people who have dared to seek human connection across the color line have often faced loss of love and standing from White family and community (16). Although a relatively small but organized group of agitators caused most of the trouble within the school, it is striking that this aggressive and separatist performance of Whiteness had so much power among students and adults alike, and in the face of that coerced silence and support, segregationists were emboldened and ultimately authorized as the voice of Little Rock's White community. "Instances of friendship" between whites and the Little Rock Nine, Melba reports, "were shrinking rather than growing" (165).

But something more is happening, too. This now unified Whiteness that is so privileged and so unrestrained is, according to Beals's narrative, becoming more unmanageable and out of control:

> Entering the door was like walking into a zoo with the animals outside their cages. The room was double the size of the largest classroom in my old school. I'd never seen anything like it or imagined in my wildest dreams that an important school like Central could allow such outrageous behavior. . . . The teacher sat meekly behind his desk, a spectator stripped of the desire or power to make them behave. (141)

Beals equates the size of the room with the importance of the school and expects a minimal level of civilized behavior. However, White students and staff were not living up to that expectation. What Beals narrates instead are scenes of chaos and disintegration within this grand space, a picture of Whiteness at war with itself—one face monstrously out of control, the other resigned and disengaged, cowered into silence and sub-mission. Lacking moral and ethical responsibility in key areas of their civic lives, these Whites embrace an even more excessive hatefulness and self-centeredness. As Thurman points out in *The Luminous Darkness*, "Hate is a funny thing. It does not have a mind. All hate knows to do is hate" (27). Here we see the fruition of that statement. The offending students were not only hostile and aggressive toward Beals but, unchecked in that behavior, they also lost all sense of propriety and respect for their white teachers as figures of authority or the classroom as a space of learning.

Once released, hate cannot be contained or directed; it becomes a central part of one's personality and threatens to infect *intra*racial relationships as much as interracial interactions. The presence of the nine African American students does very little to shift the habitual performances of Whiteness in Central High. In fact, violence, a consistent mechanism for dominating African American people, was here used in multiple ways to create a hegemonic experience of Whiteness for everyone in that space.

Central High shaped, and was shaped by, the battles that were waged to desegregate it. On the one side, African American students (and their families) who had long desired the benefits the school offered risked and sacrificed a year of their lives to take advantage of the new law of the land that had abolished "separate but equal" as the legal basis for racism in America. Within the walls and halls of Central, a new subjectivity was forged, that of "warrior," that gave them the strength to endure the chaos and madness of White racism and violence. On the other side, middle- and working-class whites found the places and privileges of Whiteness undermined not only by federal law but, more problematically for how they perceived their standing within the body of Whiteness, by local White elites, who exempted themselves from the necessity of racial reinvention through the leveraging of space to protect their own interests. Central High, now *de*segregated, was no longer a safe haven of assumed sameness. As a result, the school became a battleground in which Whiteness was created again, if not anew, through violence and terror that reasserted fictive kin groups among the disparate interests of Whiteness. White violence and the silence around it within the White community made Whiteness appear monolithic, coherent, and unified. It made the need for internal self-reflection less urgent by imposing a "we're-all-right" mentality at the very time when the force of legal and social reform was demanding a radical reenvisioning and reinvention of Whiteness. Perhaps a critical double consciousness—that ability to see oneself through the eyes of those who have been Othered—would have provided Whiteness with the means to recognize its own uses of space, place, and violence to maintain its false sense of community and identity.

Conclusion

"NO WHITE AND LEGAL HEIR"

The Responsibility of Whiteness in a Multiracial World

> From the beginning, America has been a schizophrenic nation.
> Its two conflicting images of itself were never reconciled,
> because never before has the survival of its most cherished
> myths made a reconciliation mandatory.
> —Eldridge Cleaver, *Soul on Ice*

> If we are going to build a multiracial society, which is our
> only hope, then one has got to accept that I have learned a lot
> from you, and a lot of it is bitter, but you have a lot to learn
> from me, and a lot of that will be bitter. That bitterness is
> our only hope. That is the only way we get past it.
> —James Baldwin, "The Nigger We Invent"

> Grieving is not the same as seeing the shadow in everyone but yourself.
> —Alice Walker, *Sent by Earth*

African American intellectuals have a long, rich history of critical engagement with constructions of Whiteness. From W. E. B. Du Bois's and Charles Chesnutt's interest in the psychology of Whiteness to Frank Yerby's and Zora Neale Hurston's examinations of white women's understanding and use of power in a racist patriarchy to Melba Pattillo Beals's suggestive linking of space, identity, and violence in the making of Whiteness, the literature of white estrangement has consistently excavated the meanings and costs of Whiteness for white folks. People of color have had to *know* Whiteness with an intimacy not required of white folks themselves, as a means of survival. At this juncture, twenty years and three "waves"[1] into the field of critical whiteness studies with its radical, progressive roots, there is still much that can be learned from African American interrogations and examinations of Whiteness.

Traditionally, Whiteness has been organized according to an "essentialist and non-relational understanding of identity," through the denial of connection with black and brown bodies that has served to preserve the economic and social privileges of the former group, even if individuals within Whiteness benefited unevenly (Dwyer and Jones, 210). This distance has been sustained by rhetorical and ideological scripts that dehumanize people of color by attributing all that is undesirable and fearful onto the black body, as well as legal and social sanctions that decriminalized violence against that objectified body. Simultaneously, Whiteness is mythologized as innocent, good, and free, providing a psychological cover for individuals and a cultural disincentive for whites to examine Whiteness closely, to recognize the high price that has been exacted to maintain the farce of Whiteness in our social world. James Baldwin asserts in *The Fire Next Time* that the true crime of race in the United States is that Whiteness refuses to acknowledge the destruction it has both caused and set into motion. He argues, "it is not permissible that the authors of devastation should also be innocent" (334). The literature of white estrangement does not present the picture of an unencumbered and blameless Whiteness. Rather, Whiteness in these texts is often willfully blind and indifferent to the pain that it has caused. It is the incessant and aggressive refusal to recognize the fullness of black pain—and to accept responsibility for that pain—that Chesnutt speaks to in the Viney–Malcolm Dudley subplot of *The Colonel's Dream*. No matter the apologies Dudley provides over the years, his unwillingness to acknowledge the depth of Viney's violation— the attack that he authorized as well as the pain he caused through his personal betrayal of their relationship—bars true reconciliation. It keeps them locked in a stalemate of mutual suffering: Viney unable to voice her pain or extract sentiments or behaviors from him that acknowledge her humanity; Dudley unable to forgive himself, achieve forgiveness from her, or begin to create an identity that incorporates those painful truths and that paves the way for personal transformation. The history remains alive and continues to haunt their present because Dudley avoids a full recognition of the devastation that is the price of his Whiteness. The same is true of Colonel French. His actions are predicated on his willingness to acknowledge only so much of Whiteness's responsibility for the world it has created. Redemption of the historical and continuing pain of racism and the violence and inhumanity of Whiteness is not possible when that past continues to be approached as if no one were responsible for what happened. Innocence is a privilege of Whiteness, not the basis for the repair and rebuilding that is necessary to release us from the grip of the past.

Another prong of the nonrelational epistemology of Whiteness has been the belief that Whiteness, unlike any other subject position, is forged and formed independently as the ultimate act of unencumbered self-fashioning. Whites are not members of a racial group, they are individuals; whites are not white, they are American. Thus, Whiteness fails to acknowledge or recognize the ways in which conceptions of the White self are often bound up with and juxtaposed to constructions of Blackness, Otherness, and foreignness. Whiteness is posited as the ultimate marker of "belonging" (to a community, to the nation), with all "Others" being positioned as uninvited, untolerated guests. We see this attitude in the figure of the White John in Du Bois's "Of the Coming of John," who thinks of his African American counterpart as a social interloper when he encounters him during an evening at the theater, and most clearly in the historical battles to desegregate institutions and services in the South. In these cases, as we saw more recently with the discourse of the Right during the 2008 presidential campaign season,[2] African Americans were regarded as unwanted outsiders unprepared for and undeserving of the rights and amenities of citizenship. To have people of color attaining access and positions that had formerly been reserved for Whiteness fundamentally challenged how whites understood their racial identities. Their virulent resistance highlighted the ways in which Whiteness was dependent on conceptions of an "Othered" Blackness.

The literature of white estrangement consistently unearths Whiteness's dependence on an Africanist presence to understand and construct itself. That reliance is implied in a number of minor characters in Chesnutt's *The Colonel's Dream* and in the characters of Stephen Fox and Odalie Arceneaux in Yerby's *The Foxes of Harrow*, both of whom establish their Whiteness through racial and social performances that are implicitly juxtaposed to the enslaved who also populate the community in which they live. Yerby's reworking of the Southern belle image goes so far as to posit that Whiteness is the result of a miscegenated mind that is always posturing, performing, and constituting itself in rhetorical dialogue with a Blackness that it has imagined. In all of these examples, Whiteness is demonstrated to be a relational identity. However, the mechanisms that mask and sustain Whiteness—the range of rationales and justifications that work to preserve the myth of white autonomy and independence—obscure its dependency on Blackness. Despite the investment in Whiteness as the ultimate marker of nonrelational self-fashioning, nothing could be further from the truth. The desire for complete independence and freedom is a fantasy, or perhaps a delusion, of Whiteness.

The literature of white estrangement also points to the interconnectedness of Whiteness and Blackness on another level. Although much has been and can be made of the segregation of whites and blacks, it is also true that that distance was not absolute. There was just as much proximity as there was separation, a fact that leads Diane Harriford and Becky Thompson to speak of the "twisted intimacy" of blacks and whites in the South, a claim I believe is also revealing of interracial relations outside of that particular region. "The law kept people away from each other—separate houses, schools, churches, restaurants, juke joints," they write, "to maintain the racial caste system. Existing along side of that, however, was a familiarity and a sense of connectedness that was created by complicated and emotionally intense relationships" (n.p.): relationships that were, and are, familial. Intimacy among members of that family, however, is often twisted by competing expectations of and demands on the White subject. White supremacy and racism demand not only that whites try to avoid close, personal connections with people of color but also that they exploit and profit from that larger human family that is constituted across the color line. Not to do so in a racist society has traditionally been to jeopardize one's own identification and identity, to risk losing the status and privileges of Whiteness among other, so-called Whites. Thus, while whites are encouraged to believe that Whiteness is the premier foundation for social interaction and advancement, that it is a beneficial structure that enables multiracial human communities to thrive with limited conflict, the exploitation of people of color within this mythic formulation of Whiteness, and the conformity that is required of white folks themselves if they are to remain within the protections of this White community, are never acknowledged. Whiteness has to work hard to project an image of itself as self-contained and self-sustained. White folks have to deny a certain experience of the world to imagine Whiteness as a safe haven—for anyone.

The literature of white estrangement gives voice to that which has been repressed within Whiteness. In these black-authored texts, there is often an unarticulated longing in White characters for what they have lost or turned away from: their fuller humanity, which is most often symbolized by their relationship with African American people. We see this in "Of the Coming of John," for instance. The home and community that the White John grows up in is populated by African American people; they live on the same property he does, are childhood companions, and work all around him in various circumscribed positions. Segregation has not separated folks in this community very much at all, yet it is clear that this is a community experiencing a segregation of the spirit, the failure of human recognition and regard that Thurman theorized in *The Luminous Darkness.* As the subject with more socially ascribed power in the relationship, the White John is the one with the ability to bridge this segregation of spirit; through his actions he could signal a desire to facilitate healing in this interracial community. However, the White John is only willing to *fantasize* the cross-racial acceptance and human connection for which he seems to long. His narration of racial harmony and the loving companionship of the Black John reveal his loss, but the community he desires remains beyond his reach because he chooses Whiteness over his humanity. Unable to acknowledge his loss or longing even to himself, he subconsciously seeks something that will satisfy his yearning for connection across the color line. He wanders out of his home completely agitated and restless, and when he sees Jennie, the sister of his childhood friend, he assaults her.

Coming as it does on the heels of a performance that has ensured that the White John will receive recognition and acceptance only within the white community (the lie he tells his father about the Black John), his attack on Jennie is positioned as a possible substitute for the deeper longing that he cannot safely speak or act upon. He wants to be recognized by the Black John as friend and family, wants to believe that the "cordial and intimate relations between white and black" signify something more than racial deference, but his actions make the cross-racial relationship he fantasizes impossible (Du Bois, *Souls of Black Folk,* 526). Baldwin predicted, "Nothing is more dangerous than . . . isolation, for men will commit any crimes whatever rather than endure it" ("Male Prison," 105). Left in isolation with only a white community to ground him, John becomes an even greater danger. He seeks satisfaction in the only way that is sanctioned by the narrow and limited family of Whiteness, through a violent physical union with (and domination of) Blackness. But a nonconsensual, physical encounter is not interchangeable with the kind of emotional, perhaps even spiritual, connection that John desires. He is killed at the hands of Jennie's enraged brother, the person whom he once imagined as a loving friend; the avenging John is then murdered at the hands of an irate White lynch mob. Having lacked the courage to transform himself and to act on his desire for human community and connection (as opposed to White community and acceptance), the White John is only able to solidify the *dis*union of the black and white communities.

An even more explicit tale of hypocrisy and self-delusion, longing for interracial connection, and failure of community is told in the Langston Hughes piece "Father and Son," published in his short fiction collection *The Ways of White Folks.* "Father and Son" is the story of Colonel Tom Norwood, a white plantation owner and great man of his community, and his youngest, biracial son, Bert. Their relationship, or lack thereof, is defined by the phrase, "no white and legal heir," for although Colonel Tom has lived with Bert's mother, Coralee Lewis, for more than twenty years and has fathered five children—his only children—with her, this family does not "count" (207). The colonel, and the White community in which he has standing, think of Bert as having "no relatives," and he strictly maintains racial protocols meant to reinforce his status as a White man of power even among those who should be, or could be, closest to him (248). Cora still refers to him as Colonel Tom despite their long intimacy and the fact that there "ain't been a white woman . . . overnight" at the residence since the colonel's young wife died (249). His children all have their mother's surname, and, although educated because their father both allowed and provided for it, they are forbidden to speak of their paternity. These mandates and protocols of interaction within the family enable the colonel to maintain the fiction of disconnection to himself as well as within the larger white community. For the colonel, Bert is "Cora's son," a bastard child without a legitimate home or father (240).

Hughes makes it clear that Tom Norwood's stance regarding his kin, and in particular this son who looks and acts so much like him, is a meditated, conscious performance meant to preserve his sense of his Whiteness. Colonel Tom is quietly impressed with and proud of Bert, the child who refused to obey the rules meant to separate him from his birthright as well as his human dignity. Furthermore, the colonel, like others on the plantation, is looking forward to seeing Bert when he returns from school after a six-year, forced absence. However, the colonel does not express his anticipation or joy over his son's return. While certainly some of his actions—like incessantly thinking of Bert as Cora's child and insisting that no African American person enter or leave the Big House

Plantation through the front door—result from internalized, perhaps even subconscious beliefs about race, it is also evident that much of the colonel's behavior is conscious and meditated. He spends time thinking about how he can and should "walk . . . like a white man" when he goes to the Quarters to meet his son, and closes himself off in a "small room" to "let all the Negroes in the house know that he had no interest whatsoever" in Bert's return (212, 209). He also refuses to shake his son's hand when they finally see each other again and orders Bert to work in the fields like "any other nigger on the place," both deliberate actions meant to put Bert "in his place" by impressing upon him his distance from Whiteness (231). Colonel Tom goes to great effort to ensure that his Whiteness is not compromised before others, or before himself.

Nowhere is his decision to embrace Whiteness above family better illustrated than in the beating he gives Bert as a child. While Norwood is showing horses to guests at the stable, Bert runs in to announce dinner: "Papa! . . . Papa, Ma says she's got dinner ready." The colonel "knocked him down under the feet of the horses right there in front of the guests; afterwards he . . . locked him in the stable and [beat] him severely," to teach him "not to call him papa, and certainly not in front of white people from the town" (210). Caught in the sights of his white peers, he shuns and humiliates his son, demonstrating to his guests that Bert means less to him than the horses. In this act, the colonel reveals his (white) double consciousness, his awareness of being caught in the crosshairs of at least two gazes that place compelling, but contradictory, demands on the constitution of his White self. The White gaze (represented in this scene by his guests) originates from the clan that he was born into and was taught to identify with, the group that provided home, support, and some semblance of community during his formative years. It is a gaze that demands conformity and allegiance as a prerequisite to group acceptance, even if that conformity requires disloyalty to the individual self. Thandeka explains this dynamic further:

> The actual emotional content of the term *white* . . . [is] the feeling of being
> at risk within one's own community because one has committed (or might
> commit) a communally proscribed act. . . . The child and then the adult
> learn how to suppress such risky feelings of camaraderie with persons
> beyond the community's racial pale in order to decrease the possibility of
> being exiled from their own community. And added to the loss of these feel-
> ings is the loss of self-respect resulting from discarding them. (16)

Colonel Tom privileges the regard of the white community over recognition of and connection with his black family and performs in such a way that white folks from town will not believe he values or loves the family he has created outside the bounds of Whiteness. Recognizing the potential for expulsion, he chooses to remain in the White community rather than to embrace his humanity and his family. Investing in Whiteness requires one to be on heightened alert, continually monitoring one's emotions, actions, behaviors, and thoughts for outlawed content. It is, in effect, a schizophrenic subjectivity that necessitates a betrayal of the self to reconcile oneself with the group.

The beating that followed, however, was meant to communicate something more, and to a different audience. That violence was meant to reestablish the appropriate racial hierarchy between the man and the child, a performance that was as much about the colonel's *self*-image as it was about Bert's transgressive utterance. Removed from an external White gaze, Norwood now seeks to establish an *internal* sense of his Whiteness once again, to banish the connection *he* feels to his son. However, the beating does not achieve the anticipated or desired result of establishing an insuperable distinction between White father and non-White son. The colonel does not feel more White, or more the man, by this action. Instead, the beating "always" made this patriarch "a little ashamed" (209). If shame is "a pitched battle by a self against itself in order to stop feeling what it is not supposed to feel: forbidden desires and prohibited feelings that render one different," then the shame Colonel Tom feels is evidence of a father who cares deeply for a son he cannot appear to love (Thandeka, 12).

Hughes makes clear in the story that Colonel Tom's Whiteness is nothing more, or less, than the choices he makes about who to recognize as his family. Should he decide that his family are the people whom he has loved, kept close to him, and provided for, it would open him up to a community that is right outside his door and to ways of being in the world that are not based on physical and emotional control that separates him from others. His longing for community and an end to his self-imposed exile are clear as he strolls out of his house toward the Quarters, where hears "Negroes' voices, musical and laughing." When he decides to put his Whiteness before his humanity, however, all possibility of connecting with his family is lost. As he deliberates on how to "walk through this group like a white man," their "laughter died and dripped and trickled away, and talk quieted, and silence fell degree by degree, each step the white man approached" (211–212). Choosing Whiteness not only destroys community and ensures his continued isolation but also constitutes his entry into a different clan, one premised on the denial of the fullness of one's humanity and the rejection of membership in the *human* family. The only connection among members of this clan is the violence done to "Others" to maintain the supremacy of Whiteness and the fictions of race in their world. It is a community that seems dangerous and predatory because the line of who is "outside" can shift unpredictably, because those who were once embraced can be just as easily rejected and expelled: Spick, White Trash, Nigger Lover, Faggot, Jew, Wigger, Long-Term Unemployed Worker.[3] As Baldwin writes, "They dare not trust one another. One of them may be next" ("To Crush," 165). Colonel Norwood chooses to join a community that is really no community at all.

This distancing of the White self—the denial of literal and figurative "family"—has had profound implications for efforts at inclusive citizenship in the United States. One of the long-standing rationales for a white supremacist (and patriarchal) social order has been the assertion that that foundation provides the best structure for effectively managing human difference to support the stability of communities and, ultimately, the nation. The implicit association of Whiteness with this order enabled the invisibility of Whiteness as it simply became the standard against which all other groups were compared, both rhetorically and materially. The image of the happy white family living in the harmonious, protected white community did much to communicate the idea that everything was all right in Whiteness, that there was nothing *worth* examining in this mundane normalcy. However, even when written in periods where this white fantasy was perhaps closest to being reality, the literature of white estrangement does not typically showcase an idyllic White society. Rather, what gets represented are multiracial spaces where White supremacy reigns in communities that imagine themselves as White but that are really exercising power to mask, or perhaps deny, the diversity that is their inescapable reality.

Many narratives and analyses that make up the literature of white estrangement are, or become, domestic tales set in the intimate spaces of black and white contact, the places and times in which African Americans are most often able to witness the failures and contradictions of Whiteness. In the spaces where Whiteness is accustomed to comfortable, easy movements in and through space, however, white people are easily unsettled when black folks fail to adhere to the master narratives of Blackness—when they are insistently *present*. We see this in the metaphorical meeting between the two Johns and in the actual battles that occurred in

the fifties and sixties as African Americans began the long road to claiming our human and civil rights. Beals's memoir in particular calls attention
to the metonymic relationship to place that Whiteness often develops, an
unrecognized sense of space being an extension of the White body, which
can lead to Whiteness feeling exposed in profound ways once those places
become more integrated. Perhaps this repressed psychological anxiety
also accounts for the persistent reality of segregated communities, work-
places, and educational facilities and drives contemporary manifestations
of "white flight."[4] If white people largely "do not want to be seen by the
dark Other," perhaps a fear of being caught in an oppositional gaze helps
to explain the social separation that continues to be maintained and preferred in the day-to-day lives of too many white Americans (hooks, "Representations of Whiteness," 168).

While this tradition certainly helps us to understand more fully the discourses and justifications of Whiteness at work in a particular location
and period, it also suggest ways of "reading" Whiteness that cross, or perhaps transcend, particular moments and places in history. It is this larger,
more enduring side of Whiteness, with which I end.

It's the end of the day and I'm relaxing with NPR's *All Thing Considered*. On this particular summer afternoon, I tune in toward the end of
an interview with the British historian Lord Hugh Thomas, author of *The
Golden Empire: Spain, Charles V, and the Creation of America*, who is
explaining his argument about the Spanish conquistadores' contact with,
and ultimate domination of, the Inca empire. The "beginning of the collapse of the old Incan empire," he explains, was initiated when the Spaniards massacred the king of the Incas, Atahualpa, and many of his nobles,
"on the accusation that they were plotting to destroy the Spaniards."
Thomas hardly takes a breath before continuing, "The Spaniards were very
few and they were extremely nervous, I think, and they didn't know what
they were going to do 'til the very last minute." Host Robert Siegel asks a
bit later if Thomas feels as if he knows the conquistadores about whom he
writes, to which the author replies,

> I feel they're friends, many of them, I must say, and I'm interested in where
> they came from. I'm interested to think of how these remarkable people
> who, whatever their faults, they were certainly brave, they took risks, they
> experienced enormous hardships. And it is true, I was interested in [think-
> ing] how is it possible that someone coming from small town[s] . . . in Spain,

they could spend their lives in South America, creating an empire on behalf of the king of Spain. An astounding achievement.

And there it was. Whiteness. This Englishman's words immediately took me to James Baldwin's crystallized insight, "But on the same day, in another gathering and in the most private chamber of his heart always, the white American remains proud of that history for which he does not wish to pay, and from which, materially, he has profited so much" ("Guilt," 411). Not American here, but the same spirit. Pride. I squirmed; my skin prickled. Then, as if sensing my discomfort or recognizing an oddness in Lord Thomas's celebration of this history of genocidal conquest, Siegel follows up by noting that recent publications on the Spanish conquest of the Americas have been "far less sympathetic" than Thomas's retelling of the story. He asks, "What's right here? How should we view this?" The author chimes in,

> We must certainly recognize it was an astounding achievement. I recognize that they were brutal and sometimes contradictory. Sometimes foolish. But still, I'm . . . I admire their achievement more than I condemn it. But an important point which I mention quite a lot in this book is the Spaniards discussed as to whether they had any rights to be in the New World . . . was there any justification for their conquests? And I think I emphasize the fact that in no other imperial history . . . do we see such a discussion of this nature. I mean, my father was in Africa all his life, he was a good man, but he never wondered why he was there. He never thought, "Well, we must have a discussion with the Africans as to whether we have a right to be here."

In the space of an eight-minute interview, listeners were taken on a journey into the psychology, the soul, of Whiteness. We were asked, expected, to view the events of history from the vantage point of the invading Spaniards, those "remarkable people" who executed a nation's leadership to establish themselves in a "new world." We are told that, "whatever their faults," they were brave men who acted more from a sense of their own vulnerability than out of malice. *They* took risks, *they* sacrificed; they, Lord Thomas intimates, are to be *admired* for their success in establishing the Spanish empire on another continent and for their successful domination of the indigenous nations that they encountered. And then, the deeply buried source of Thomas's pride and his refusal to judge the brutal actions of an invading army is revealed: Lord Thomas's father was an imperial agent in Africa. "My father . . . was a good man."

"My father . . . was a good man" is an extraordinary statement given the fact that the elder Thomas "never wondered why he was there." It is a deliberate turning away from, an erasure of, the atrocities of colonial (and domestic) histories. In this statement, Thomas claims and seeks to recuperate the murdering conquistadores—those White folks who feel like his friends, who could have been people he knew growing up—and his settler-colonial father, from their choices and their actions. It is a denial of that "other" family, that larger, human family, that was, and is, decimated each time Whiteness tells itself that "good people" can act in these ways and still remain innocent.

The literature of white estrangement issues a sociological imperative to remake the world, and a spiritual imperative to create one in which human recognition and community are possible. It also speaks to the need for a particular history of Whiteness not only to be recovered and critically engaged but also to be redeemed. Perhaps it is disheartening to realize that so much of what was said in the nineteenth and twentieth centuries about Whiteness still applies and is still revealing, but it is also promising to realize that we have not reached the limit of our understanding, nor have we exhausted our means of teaching to transgress the structures that have kept race so entrenched in the United States. Like the White John and Colonel Norwood, White Americans dimly sense their loss and desire for something more, yet their investment in the racial social order of their communities works to repress the knowledge of the choices they have made and the parts of themselves they have to close off in order to be at home in Whiteness. White double consciousness is this mind—Du Bois would say "soul"—divided against itself, feverishly erecting defenses to prevent the emergence of true self-consciousness and the heavy responsibility of personal transformation that often attends such self-awareness. Sometimes, however, something, or someone, intervenes and the sleep-walker awakens.[5]

The literature of white estrangement is an intellectual tradition and body of work that is thoughtful and deliberate in its engagement with Whiteness. Its analyses are historically situated, strategic interventions in the politics of Whiteness, an oppositional gaze that challenges the narratives and myths used to uphold, justify, and rationalize White supremacy as a legitimate sociopolitical foundation in the United States and beyond. In this way, the literature of white estrangement has been an important tool in the arsenals of African American intellectuals attempting to create a society in which the promise and dignity of all people is recognized and honored. However, this tradition also does more. It bears witness to the insecurity, instability, fear, and loss that is both the cause and the result of Whiteness. It is a vantage point that calls attention not only to the compromises and lapses of the *individual*, the distance between how Whites want to live their lives and the lives they actually live, but also to the *social* inconsistencies, contradictions, and failures of Whiteness. Here, the literature of white estrangement attempts to function as a moral barometer or conscience, emphasizing to White Americans the tangible losses of self, morality, and human connection that are the casualties of investing in Whiteness as it has been traditionally constructed. It is a gaze that holds whites accountable for the devastation that race has and continues to play in the United States, but also reminds Whiteness of choices it *could* make to redeem its past, correct its present, and create a more just future. If white Americans would only respond to the appeal of this gaze with "silence and humility," they could recreate Whiteness by finding the courage to act from a liberalizing sense of who they could be (Yancy, 13).

Thinking broadly about the potential of this oppositional gaze to counter oppressive and exploitative performances of Whiteness suggests an even more powerful way of proceeding, namely to imagine Whiteness as a Creolized identity, as Frank Yerby did in *The Foxes of Harrow.* "Creolized" would be an apt way of naming a radical white subjectivity that is willing to embrace the darkness within itself as a metaphor for the internalization of this oppositional black gaze, a vantage point that would enable it to estrange traditional performances of Whiteness and to develop a critical white double consciousness that would effectively counter white schizophrenic subjectivity. Armed with the deep knowledge of the histories and mechanisms of Whiteness available in the literature of white estrangement, this reenvisioned, reformed, Creolized Whiteness would be less likely to slide unreflectively, unknowingly, into white moderation as the ideal psychological position for whites. Embracing *this* gaze could lead to an interracial healing that has long eluded us.

NOTES

INTRODUCTION

1. I first introduced this term in the article "Lillian B. Horace and the Literature of White Estrangement."

2. To date, only three critical texts have been published that deal substantially with texts from the literature of white estrangement tradition. The earliest collection is David Roediger's *Black on White: Black Writers on What It Means to Be White* (1998). That same year, Claudia Tate published *Psychoanalysis and Black Novels: Desire and the Protocols of Race*, which critically engages several novels from the tradition, including Richard Wright's *Savage Holiday* and Zora Neale Hurston's *Seraph on the Suwanee*. In 2006, Gene Andrew Jarrett published *African American Literature Beyond Race: An Alternative Reader*, which presented complete works or substantial excerpts from sixteen understudied, noncanonical texts that could be considered part of the tradition I am identifying. According to Jarrett, "less than 2 percent of all the dissertations, articles, chapters in edited collections, and books published . . . since 1963" have been devoted to the titles in his anthology (9).

3. Both Hughes and Hurston are part of a long tradition in which African American writers critique the sociopolitical contexts for Black writing and the role of the artist and intellectual in the African American and American cultures. See in particular Langston Hughes's "The Negro Artist and the Racial Mountain," Zora Neale Hurston's "What White Publishers Won't Print," and Ralph Ellison's "Brave Words for a Startling Occasion." These and other essays that take up these questions and debates are included in Winston Napier's edited volume, *African American Literary Theory*.

4. See Gates's essay, "Mister Jefferson and the Trials of Phillis Wheatley," in which he recounts the tribunal that was held to determine whether the enslaved author Phillis Wheatley had authored the collection of poems she claimed as hers. Gates's analysis leads him to conclude that African American writing emerged from and responded to a particularly racialized and politicized context. He asserts that Jefferson's charge that black writing was merely imitative and derivative served as a catalyst for black literary and critical production for generations. Further, however, Gates claims that critical responses to Wheatley's work at various historical moments were a means of setting guidelines and expectations for African American writing, for writers and readers alike.

5. The term "disappeared" is typically used in international human rights contexts to refer to people who have been abducted or imprisoned by a political organization, party, or regime who then denies any knowledge of the person's whereabouts. While I do not mean to imply a seamless parallel between the repression of the literature of

white estrangement and more violent acts of political repression, I do purposefully invoke the term to call attention to the fact that "discounting and suppressing the knowledge of whiteness held by people of color was not just a byproduct of white supremacy but an imperative of racial domination" (Roediger, 6). Racial politics have indeed undergirded decisions about how to value this intellectual tradition.

6. The literature of white estrangement actually offers some rich insights into Whiteness as an international phenomenon, as expressed through colonialism and imperialism in particular. For this book, however, I have chosen to limit my focus to the critiques and interventions that this tradition has made into constructions of Whiteness in the United States.

CHAPTER ONE

The quotation in the chapter title is taken from James Baldwin, *Notes of a Native Son* (Boston: Beacon Press, 1984): 173.

1. For discussions of whiteness and philosophy, see George Yancy's *What White Looks Like* and *Look, A White!*, Shannon Sullivan's *Revealing Whiteness*, and the work of Charles Mills, especially *The Racial Contract*. For discussions of the intersections of whiteness and the economy, see Matt Wray's *Not Quite White*, Steve Martinot's *The Machinery of Whiteness*, and the work of the labor historian David Roediger. Charles Mills also persuasively argues for the interconnectedness of religion and white supremacy in the founding of the United States, as do James Baldwin and Thandeka. *Reforging the White Republic* by Edward Blum is particularly useful for considering the ways that Christianity was employed to unify regional whiteness after the Civil War. A particularly sharp analysis of the impact of white racial constructs on empirical science fields can be found in *The Mismeasure of Man* by Stephen Jay Gould.

2. The body of scholarship that examines the psychologies and emotional lives of whites is growing. Toni Morrison's *Playing in the Dark* and Ruth Frankenberg's *White Women, Race Matters* are two of the earlier scholarly models for this type of inquiry. Others who have continued this work include historian Jason Sokol (*There Goes My Everything*), sociologist Karyn McKinney (*Being White*), theologian Thandeka (*Learning to Be White*), as well as activist Tim Wise and psychologist Lisa B. Spanierman, several of whose works are relevant. My work seeks to bring an even larger range of voices to the conversation by recovering the writing of African Americans who have pursued this line of analysis since the nineteenth century.

3. When trying to establish the lineage of Du Bois's use of the term "double consciousness," the two intellectuals pointed to most often are Ralph Waldo Emerson and William James. Other nineteenth-century thinkers and writers who utilized the term include George Eliot, S. Weir Mitchell, Henry James, and John Greenleaf Whittier. For further discussion, see also Dickson Bruce's "W. E. B. Du Bois and the

Idea of Double Consciousness" and Susan Wells's "Discursive Mobility and Double Consciousness in S. Weir Mitchell and W. E. B. Du Bois."

4. As is the case with Du Bois's theorizing of black double consciousness, White double consciousness—those sets of beliefs, norms, expectations, and often behaviors related to how whites are encouraged to think of themselves in relation and comparison to other racial groups—is both pervasive and narrowly scripted. I have chosen to capitalize "White" in this phrase to call attention to it as something into which the white racial group is broadly, and often unconsciously, socialized. The term also allows us to recognize that socialization process as related to but distinct from the choices that individual whites might make about how to understand and perform their racial identities.

5. Although blood donor programs were established during the 1920s, there was no reliable way to "bank" blood in the United States until African American surgeon and prominent researcher of blood collection and storage, Dr. Charles R. Drew, created reliable protocols, training, and facilities for collecting and storing donated blood in the late 1930s and early 1940s. Many early donor programs did not accept blood from African Americans, a restriction that was in place until 1942 when the American Red Cross announced that it would begin to process African American blood donations, but that the blood would also be segregated. Dr. Drew spoke out against blood segregation by arguing that there was no scientific evidence that blood carried markers that limited its cross-racial use. He stated in his Spingarn Medal acceptance speech in 1944, "It is fundamentally wrong for any great nation to willfully discriminate against such a large group of its people. . . . One can say quite truthfully that on the battlefields nobody is very interested in where the plasma comes from when they are hurt. . . . It is unfortunate that such a worthwhile scientific bit of work should have been hampered by such stupidity" (U.S. National Library of Medicine, "Becoming the Father").

6. In *Making Us Crazy*, Herb Kutchins and Stuart A. Kirk provide a useful overview of how race and ethnicity have historically inflected psychological testing and diagnoses. They point out that prior to the mid 1850s, few physicians believed that the enslaved were susceptible to mental illness, due largely to skewed tests and data that supported a priori assumptions about the "cranial inadequacies" of African Americans (209). The few disorders that were attributed to enslaved Blacks—such as drapetomania, a mental disease that caused slaves to run away, and dysaesthesia aethiopis, a disorder that led slaves to be lazy and to destroy things—supported the social expectations for their behavior. The heavy responsibility of freedom was also thought to cause mental illness in African Americans.

7. For a fuller discussion of the convict lease system as a tool of social control of African Americans in the Reconstruction era, see chapter 1 of Michelle Alexander's *The New Jim Crow: Mass Incarceration in the Age of Colorblindness*.

8. Of the generation of historians who routinely represented Reconstruction as a failed social experiment and the leaders of the Confederate cause as misunderstood

freedom fighters, see the work of William Woodward, John W. Burgess, William A. Dunning, Claude G. Bowers, and James Ford Rhodes.

9. The "New South" was a term coined in the post-Reconstruction era to invoke the vision of a prosperous and urbanized South. It was used as a rallying call for the South to reform and reimagine itself as a more modern, regional counterpart to the North after the Civil War. However, New South proponents such as Paul Gaston and Henry Grady asserted that even as the South sought to lift itself out of poverty through industrialization, it should hold onto its distinctively "Southern culture," which was marked by its investment in a White supremacist racial creed and its repudiation of the anonymity and abuses of capitalism in favor of agrarian life.

10. A similar motivation exists in the case of another prisoner, Bud Johnson, with whom the colonel's story becomes entangled. Although he had witnessed Johnson being sold and had recoiled from the "customs" of the South, it is not until he realizes that Johnson is married to his fiancé's servant that he takes action (Chesnutt, *Dream*, 68). He is unwilling to intervene unless he, personally, can benefit by doing so. In this case, his intervention reaffirms his opinion of himself as a good man with the "beneficent power to scatter happiness" (241).

11. According to Suzanne Poirier, author of "The Weir Mitchell Rest Cure: Doctor and Patients," Mitchell, who developed the treatment, did occasionally prescribe it for men. But it is clear that the cure was most often recommended for women, as it was the standard treatment for diagnoses of both hysteria and nervous prostration in women, quickly supplanting pelvic surgery as the most common response to these "disorders." See also Michael Blackie's article, "Reading the Rest Cure."

CHAPTER TWO

The quotation in the chapter title is taken from Frank Yerby, *The Foxes of Harrow* (Garden City, N.Y.: Sun Dial Press, 1946): 129

1. One of the earlier readings to comment on the culpability and contradictory positioning of the white moderate is *The Negro Novel in America* by Robert Bone. Louis Graham examines a larger number of white moderate characters, including Richard Wright's Jan Erlone and Boris Max, in his essay "The White Self-Image Conflict in *Native Son*." Both conclude that although Wright's white characters see themselves, and want to be seen, as racial progressives, their inability to examine their own investments in whiteness prevent them from acknowledging their "true identit[ies] as oppressor[s]" (Graham, 20).

2. The term "Cult of True Womanhood" was coined by Barbara Welter in 1966 in her article "The Cult of True Womanhood, 1820–1860." Since then, hundreds of books, articles, and dissertations have been penned on the topic, expanding, challenging, and reassessing Welter's basic premise that nineteenth-century women conformed themselves to, and were judged by their adherence to, a strict cultural

script of womanhood: the "four cardinal virtues [of] piety, purity, submissiveness and domesticity" that defined True Womanhood (152). Of note are scholars like Susan Cruea and Carroll Smith-Rosenberg, who extend Welter's work to analyze women's roles and responsibilities *outside* of the home, suggesting, as Cruea states directly, that the Cult recognized in women a "moral authority which implicitly empowered them to extend their moral influence outside the home. . . . many women asserted that it was their duty to spread . . . guidance outside the home as well, in order to protect their families and improve the public good" (190).

3. Women Accepted for Volunteer Emergency Service (WAVES) served in the navy in a broad range of positions, including the aviation, medical, and communications fields. According to the U.S. Navy's web pages on "Naval History and Heritage," within a year of the WAVES program being authorized, 27,000 women were in uniform. SPARs was the nickname for the Coast Guard Women's Reserve (the acronym is taken from the Coast Guard motto in Latin, "semper paratus," and English, "always ready"). Robin Thomson records that more than 10,000 women volunteered for service as SPARs between 1942 and 1946. The 150,000 women who served in the U.S. Army were members of the Women's Army Corps (WAC). All three divisions were authorized by Congress in 1942.

4. These were the female protagonists of three popular films of the period: *Laura* (1944), *Gilda* (1946), and *Gone with the Wind* (1939). Each lead actress—Gene Tierney, Rita Hayworth, and Vivian Leigh, respectively—saw her industry and popular appeal skyrocket after her performance in the aforementioned films.

5. The Double V campaign was unofficially launched in 1942 when James G. Thompson wrote a letter to the *Pittsburgh Courier* questioning why African Americans were enlisting to fight for "victory over aggression, slavery, and tyranny" abroad when they still faced discrimination, oppression, and prejudice at home and in the armed forces. He called for African Americans to "adopt the double VV for a double victory over our enemies within," arguing that "those who perpetuate these ugly prejudices here are seeking to destroy our democratic form of government just as surely as the axis forces" (quoted in Phillips, 24). His critical questioning became the basis of a national campaign by black Americans to actively challenge the mistreatment and disrespect African American servicemen and servicewomen faced in the American military, and to challenge the racist violence and segregation endured by black Americans in all walks of life. For a fuller discussion of the strategies for resistance employed during the campaign, see Kimberly Phillips's *War! What Is It Good For?*

6. Charlene Regester provides an excellent discussion of African American–authored narratives adapted to film prior to 1950 in "African-American Writers and Pre-1950 Cinema."

7. Morrison makes this assertion most concisely in the article "On the Backs of Blacks." There, analyzing a scene from Elia Kazan's film *America*, she notes that the Greek immigrant's dismissal of and scorn for an African American character "transforms this charming Greek into an entitled white. Without it [his racial contempt], Stavros' future as an American is not at all assured" (145).

Notes

8. Plaçage was a formalized (although not legally recognized) arrangement that enabled interracial relationships between wealthy white men and free, mixed-race women in antebellum New Orleans. From the arrangement, the plaçée, as she was known, derived economic security, social status, and relative freedom in the highly racialized South. In return, she effectively surrendered her freedom to her white partner, making him "both master and lover" (Li, 67). The relationships could often be of considerable duration, both preceding and, on occasion, continuing through the legal, intraracial marriage of the white patron. Children of the union were often educated and, at times, freed. For a thorough analysis of archival sources relevant to plaçage unions, see Kenneth Aslakson's "The 'Quadroon-Plaçage' Myth of Antebellum New Orleans."

9. The story of Achilles and La Belle Sauvage, two people enslaved by Stephen Fox, runs parallel that of the Foxes. The two couples are "wed" on the same day, and each husband is eagerly anticipating the consummation of his marriage. Both wives are unwilling or reluctant partners, although for different reasons. But where Stephen Fox restrains himself from raping, his African American counterpart, Achilles, does not. The implicit comparison drawn between the two men, and Stephen's restraint in circumstances similar to those faced by his manservant, marks him as White and superior to the unrestrained Black masculinity represented by Achilles.

10. Hurston also addresses another point through Jim's interaction with Joe Kelsey at this moment, namely the ways in which Whiteness relies on a dark counterpart (Morrison would say "Africanist presence") to make meaning of itself. Kelsey is known for his Saturday night exploits of "likker and women" (44). Jim is temperate and has a singular devotion to Arvay from the beginning of their courtship. Joe is willing to sacrifice the needs of his family to satisfy his own desires; Jim is the ultimate patriarch working to provide for his family. Hurston illustrates here how the stereotypes of immoderate Black masculinity help to structure White masculinity as control and mastery.

11. Foucault's major treatises on the working of power in human history include *Madness and Civilization*, *The Birth of the Clinic*, *Discipline and Punish*, and *The History of Sexuality*. See specifically his essay "The Subject and Power."

12. For a fuller discussion of the ways in which the Africanist presence has structured White American sensibility and U.S. nation building, see Toni Morrison's *Playing in the Dark*.

13. Richard Dyer offers a compelling argument about how the white, gendered body is and has been represented in art, film, photography, and other visual media in his book *White*. Often, he asserts, the white male body is presented as the ideal body: "built . . . achieved . . . worked at, planned, suffered for" (153). This sculpted body, which hearkens back to Greek male statuary, makes an implicit connection between "bodily superiority" and the social ascendency of Whiteness. Dyer writes, "The possibility of white bodily inferiority falls heavily on the shoulders of those white men who are not at the top of the spirit pile, those for whom their body is their only capital . . . particularly white working-class or 'underachieving' masculinity" (147).

Notes

14. Published in 1936, *Gone with the Wind* was an instant popular success and won the Pulitzer Prize in 1937. It was adapted and released as an equally successful film in 1939. By the end of the 1940s, the novel had sold approximately eight million copies globally and had been translated into thirty languages. No novel of the Reconstruction South has left a bigger shadow for aspiring authors of historical fiction or a larger imprint on the imagination of readers and scholars of Southern fiction.

CHAPTER THREE

The quotation in the chapter title is taken from Melba Pattillo Beals, *Warriors Don't Cry: A Searing Memoir of the Battle to Integrate Little Rock's Central High* (New York: Simon & Schuster, 1994): 128.

1. The legal doctrine of "separate but equal" was established most famously in the *Plessy v. Ferguson* case decided by the U.S. Supreme Court in 1896. This ruling upheld the constitutionality of racial segregation as long as "equal" facilities were provided for groups classified as "non-white."

2. John A. Kirk provides a compelling analysis of Faubus's decision to support segregation as a means of advancing his political career in Chapter 5 of *Redefining the Color Line*.

3. A key distinction in geography is that which exists between space and place. According to Edward Relph, space is "amorphous and intangible . . . [it] provides the context for places" (2). Place, as Tim Cresswell succinctly defines it, is "space invested with meaning in the context of power" (*Place: Short Introduction*, 12).

4. The "surprise" I refer to here is evidenced in the ways that scholars preface and situate their discussion of the desegregation crisis in Little Rock. I regularly encountered arguments in the work of established as well as emerging historians of the event that "despite the massive resistance" movement that came together there, the city was known for its "moderate" stance toward race and for being a "progressive" area within the South. Some, clearly favoring the point of view of white Southerners in Little Rock, even assert that "race relations were considered good and improving" (Lorraine Gates, 194). See the work of Karen Anderson, John Kirk, and Lorraine Gates, quoted here.

5. For a careful statistical analysis of the composition of the crowds that surrounded Central High School in 1957, see Graeme Cope's article, "'Everybody says all those people . . . were from out of town, but they weren't': A Note on Crowds during the Little Rock Crisis." Of particular interest is his break with traditional understandings of the mobs that surrounded the school. Cope concludes that around half of the protesters were residents of Pulaski County, where Central is located, while another 38 percent resided in one of two nearby counties (256). Additionally, he finds that "those in the streets represented the middle to lower (but not the lowest) rungs of Arkansas society" (264). Both of these conclusions run counter to previous analyses asserting that the crowds were mostly lower-class "outsiders" to the community.

6. Broadly speaking, interrogations of White violence have fallen into one of two camps. Sociohistorical approaches tend to focus on violence that is enacted within a particular period and region/location, such as the Reconstruction-era South, the Civil Rights period in Mississippi and Georgia, or Watts (Los Angeles) in 1965. The force of these analyses is that they bring back to life the historical contexts of particular periods in which White violence was prevalent, helping us to understand more fully the mindsets, worldviews, and national and community mores that foreshadowed a specific white assault and determined the responses that that violence would engender. Recent studies that fall under this rubric include Cynthia Nevels's *Lynching to Belong: Claiming Whiteness through Racial Violence*, George Lewis's *Massive Resistance: The White Response to the Civil Rights Movement*, and Charles Lane's *The Day Freedom Died: The Colfax Massacre, The Supreme Court, and the Betrayal of Reconstruction*. These pieces focus on the mood of a time—the national and regional events that shaped participants' understandings of themselves and others.

A second group of studies focuses on particular types of violence, like lynching or race riots, examining them across historical time periods, geographic locations, and sociopolitical contexts. The primary goal of this scholarship is to deepen the complexity with which these events are understood by offering additional critical and theoretical approaches to a particular type of white violence. These analyses invite us to consider everything from the significance of gender to the role of economics in a particular type of violence, and utilize emerging theoretical tools as well as more established ones in their analyses. The strength of these studies is that they challenge entrenched understandings of the causes and impacts of White violence. *Southern Horrors: Women and the Politics of Rape and Lynching* by Crystal Feimster and *Buried in the Bitter Waters: The Hidden History of Racial Cleansing in America* by Elliot Jaspin are recent additions to the substantial body of work that examines particular manifestations of white violence.

7. There is a rich body of material that engages White violence in the intellectual tradition of the literature of white estrangement. Full discussion of those authors and texts is not possible here, but they include antebellum authors such as Frederick Douglass, David Walker, and William J. Wilson (Ethiop); twentieth-century activists like Ida B. Wells-Barnett, Walter White, Howard Thurman, Malcolm X, and James Baldwin; and scholars such as Charles Johnson and John Hope Franklin. The list of literary texts from this tradition that engage the topic is simply too long to recount, and they have not yet been examined specifically in terms of their portrayals of white violence during particular historical time periods.

8. I borrow this term from Charles Mills's *The Racial Contract*, wherein he argues that an "'epistemological' contract" centered around race undergirds the social and moral contracts that govern interactions between individuals and the state as well as between individual persons. While Mills asserts that the "Racial Contract is not a contract to which the nonwhite subset of humans can be a genuinely consenting party,"

he does recognize, as I do in my use of the term, that people of color often acquiesce to the contract to avoid violent consequences for their resistance (11–12).

9. The response of everyday white Southerners to the pressures of the Civil Rights movement is discussed extensively in Jason Sokol's *There Goes My Everything: White Southerners in the Age of Civil Rights, 1945–1975*. He argues that White Southerners' process of adapting to and accepting change during this period was vexed, complicated, contradictory at times, and gradual. If there was a "mind of the South" at this time, it was distinguished only by its marked confusion and pain at the adjustments it was forced to make.

10. Analyses of class differences among Little Rock's white communities and the difference they made to the desegregation crisis are numerous. See, for example, Karen Anderson's "The Little Rock School Desegregation Crisis: Moderation and Social Conflict"; she writes that small business owners and working-class people "were very wary of the class privilege and power wielded by the city's elites" (605). C. Fred Williams notes that because Superintendent Blossom "talked only to the business and professional class . . . the board's intentions did not appear innocent" to those in the working-class districts of Little Rock (342). See also Anderson's *Little Rock: Race and Resistance at Central High School*, David Chappell's "Diversity within a Racial Group: White People in Little Rock," and Pete Daniel's *Lost Revolutions: The South in the 1950s*.

11. In "The Ballot or the Bullet," Malcolm X makes the bold claim that "the white man is more afraid of separation than he is of integration." Continuing, he argues, "Segregation means that he puts you away from him, but not far enough for you to be out of his jurisdiction; separation means you're gone. And the white man will integrate faster than he'll let you separate" (42). Implicit in his claim that blacks are not "out of . . . [the] jurisdiction" of whites is Malcolm X's understanding that considerable spatial and social interaction exists among whites and blacks despite arguments in favor of segregation during his time. Blacks are not "gone" or separated to such an extent that they are allowed to exercise self-control or autonomy. Rather, as Charles Johnson asserts in his report *Patterns of Negro Segregation*, the "social implications of certain types of contact" are what determine how comfortable white people are with proximity and social contact between whites and blacks (208). Segregation is "symbolic and . . . to be understood with reference to what . . . [it] symbolize[s] rather than as an exact blueprint of personal or social action" (220).

12. In *In Place/Out of Place*, Cresswell devotes a chapter to the concept of heretical geography, which is both an understanding of place as the "result of tensions between different meanings" as well as an acknowledgment that places are "active players in these tensions" (59). My use of the term is meant to call attention to the geographical counterimagination that often exists even as those with the power to define assert exclusionary meanings of spaces, places, and the bodies that inhabit them. The meanings of spaces and places are rarely uncontested; "places have more than one meaning" (Cresswell, *In Place/Out of Place*, 59).

13. Another way of thinking about this dynamic emerges when we recognize that assumptions about space changed dramatically during this ideological conflict. Cresswell writes that when conflict arises over the use and meaning of space, "formally assumed normative geography" suddenly has to be argued and justified, has to be "made explicit." This changes "the link between spatial context and behavior . . . from an *assumed, natural, common-sense, and unquestioned* relationship to a *demanded, normal, and established* relationship that has been questioned" (*In Place/Out of Place*, 49). Political and legal arguments for desegregation disturbed the normative assumptions underpinning racial separation and implicitly challenged assertions of White superiority and Black inferiority. The need to argue for the continuation of segregation meant that the worldview that asserted racial separation as "natural" could no longer be taken for granted.

14. "Mammy" has been a stock figure in American literature and culture since the early nineteenth century. This stereotyped figure, meant to represent the historical reality of enslaved black women serving as wet nurses and caretakers for white children, became widely recognized in the 1840s and 1850s as a stock character in both pro- and antislavery antebellum plantation fiction. Roughly a century later she was immortalized in the print and film versions of *Gone with the Wind*. Kimberly Wallace-Sanders accurately points out in *Mammy: A Century of Race, Gender, and Southern Memory* that the defining characteristics of the figure are her devotion and obedience and her "maternal role for both enslaved and slave-holding families" (8). It is in her role as faithful caretaker of white America, though, that we see the intersection of race and gender in the White imagination most clearly. As a controlling image for conceptions of Black womanhood and femininity, the figure of the Mammy sought to minimize the influence black women had over white children, to dissemble the physical and sexual presence of black women within the White home, and to neutralize the political awareness and agency of the group.

CONCLUSION

The quotation in the chapter title is taken from Langston Hughes, "Father and Son," in *The Ways of White Folks* (New York: Vintage Books, 1990): 207.

1. Several scholars have argued that critical whiteness studies is best understood, like feminism, in terms of the shifts in critical concerns that have happened within the field over time. The metaphor of "waves" is used to identify these transitions. Here I agree with Charles Gallagher and France Winddance Twine, editors of *Retheorizing Race and Whiteness in the 21st Century*, that critical whiteness studies is currently in its third wave of development, although I would perhaps articulate a different set of primary concerns that have defined the field since its inception.

Notes

2. During the 2008 presidential campaign and the first year of the Obama presidency, pundits and critics freely interjected racially loaded speech and personal attacks into the public debate around nearly every initiative on the president's agenda. Some of the most egregious political cartoons featured a simian Obama, or clothed him in iconic Muslim garb like the abaya, kufi, *smagh*, or turban. The health care reform effort was referred to by one right-wing talk show host as "reparations for black people" when it was initially proposed, and the Patient Protection and Affordable Care Act of 2010 is now routinely labeled "Obamacare" by commentators on both sides of the political spectrum. More than three years into his presidency, questions about Obama's citizenship still make their way into national discourse despite the fact that the long form of his birth certificate was released in April 2011. The continual suggestion is that Obama is a dangerous, foreign outsider who has infiltrated and is working to undermine the United States.

3. One of the more recent groups to join people of color in having bleak employment prospects are middle-class workers displaced during the global economic downturn of 2009. According to Catherine Rampell, employers now are regularly refusing to hire job applicants of any race or ethnicity who are unemployed (n.p.). Although clearly the practice disproportionately impacts people of color, whose unemployment rates run higher than those of whites in the United States, it also potentially creates a new white underclass—the long-term unemployed. Whereas in previous recessions, white working professionals and midlevel managers were relatively insulated from loss of employment—the last to be fired and first to be rehired—the current downturn coupled with the practice of hiring only those currently employed is evidence that another group of white folks are now excluded from the benefits and privileges of Whiteness.

4. "White flight" refers to the out-migration of whites from a community that is experiencing an increase of African Americans and/or other people of color into the area. For further discussion, see "The Racial Context of White Mobility: An Individual-Level Assessment of the White Flight Hypothesis" by Kyle Crowder and *There Goes the Neighborhood: Racial, Ethnic, and Class Tensions in Four Chicago Neighborhoods and Their Meaning for America* by William Julius Wilson and Richard Taub.

5. In Ralph Ellison's *Invisible Man*, the moment of contact between the white sleepwalker and the invisible black subject is one fraught with danger. I offer the allusion here, however, to invoke a hopefulness that we can imagine strategic interventions that will initiate the process of awakening for more white Americans. With its pointed yet compassionate renderings of the failures of Whiteness, the literature of white estrangement may be uniquely positioned to help us reach that goal.

WORKS CITED

Ahmed, Sara. "A Phenomenology of Whiteness." *Feminist Theory* 8.2 (2007): 149–168.

Alexander, Michelle. *The New Jim Crow: Mass Incarceration in the Age of Colorblindness.* New York: The New Press, 2010.

Anderson, Karen. *Little Rock: Race and Resistance at Central High School.* Princeton: Princeton University Press, 2009.

———. "The Little Rock School Desegregation Crisis: Moderation and Social Conflict." *Journal of Southern History* 70.3 (August 2004): 603–636.

Aslakson, Kenneth. "The 'Quadroon-Plaçage' Myth of Antebellum New Orleans: Anglo-American (Mis)interpretations of a French-Caribbean Phenomenon." *Journal of Social History* 45.3 (Spring 2012): 709–734.

Baldwin, James. *The Cross of Redemption: Uncollected Writings.* Edited by Randall Kenan. New York: Pantheon Books, 2010.

———. *The Price of the Ticket: Collected Nonfiction, 1948–1985.* New York: St. Martin's/ Marek, 1985.

———. *The Fire Next Time.* In *The Price of the Ticket*, 333–379.

———. "The Male Prison." In *The Price of the Ticket*, 101–105.

———. "The Nigger We Invent." In *The Cross of Redemption*, 89–97.

———. "On Being White . . . and Other Lies." In *The Cross of Redemption*, 135–138.

———. "To Crush a Serpent." In *The Cross of Redemption*, 158–165.

———. "White Man's Guilt." In *The Price of the Ticket*, 409–414.

———. "The White Problem." In *The Cross of Redemption*, 72–79.

Bates, Daisy. *The Long Shadow of Little Rock: A Memoir.* New York: David McKay Company, 1962.

Beals, Melba Pattillo. *Warriors Don't Cry: A Searing Memoir of the Battle to Integrate Little Rock's Central High.* New York: Simon & Schuster, 1994.

Beard, George M. *American Nervousness: Its Causes and Consequences.* Reprint edition, with an introduction by Charles E. Rosenberg. New York: Arno Press, 1972. First published 1881 by G. P. Putnam's Sons.

Berg, Barbara J. *The Remembered Gate: Origins of American Feminism.* New York: Oxford University Press, 1978.

Birth of a Nation, The. Directed by D. W. Griffith. David W. Griffith Corp., 1915.

Blackie, Michael. "Reading the Rest Cure." *Arizona Quarterly* 60.2 (Summer 2004): 57–85.

Blum, Edward J. *Reforging the White Republic: Race, Religion, and American Nationalism, 1865–1898.* Baton Rouge: Louisiana State University Press, 2005.

Bone, Robert A. *The Negro Novel in America.* New Haven: Yale University Press, 1958.

Works Cited

Bonnett, Alastair. "Constructions of 'Race,' Place and Discipline: Geographies of 'Racial' Identity and Racism." *Ethnic and Racial Studies* 19.4 (October 1996): 864–883.

Bruce, Dickson, Jr. "W. E. B. Du Bois and the Idea of Double Consciousness." *American Literature* 64.2 (June 1992): 299–309.

Butcher, Philip. "Our Raceless Writers." *Opportunity: Journal of Negro Life* 26.3 (Summer 1948): 113–115.

Cash, W. J. *The Mind of the South.* 1941. New York: Vintage Books, 1991.

Chafe, William H. *The American Woman: Her Changing Social, Economic, and Political Role, 1920–1970.* New York: Oxford University Press, 1974.

Chancer, Lynn S. "Rethinking Domestic Violence in Theory and Practice." *Deviant Behavior* 25.3 (May-June 2004): 255–275.

———. *Sadomasochism in Everyday Life: The Dynamics of Power and Powerlessness.* New Brunswick: Rutgers University Press, 1992.

Chappell, David. "Diversity within a Racial Group: White People in Little Rock." *Arkansas Historical Quarterly* 66.2 (Summer 2007): 181–193.

Chesnutt, Charles. *The Colonel's Dream.* 1905. New York: Harlem Moon, 2005.

———. *The House Behind the Cedars.* 1900. Athens: University of Georgia Press, 2000.

———. *The Journals of Charles W. Chesnutt.* Edited by Richard Brodhead. Durham: Duke University Press, 1993.

———. *The Marrow of Tradition.* 1901. New York: Bedford/St. Martins, 2002.

Child, Lydia Maria. Introduction to *Incidents in the Life of a Slave Girl*, by Harriet Jacobs, 5–6. 1861. New York: W. W. Norton, 2001.

Christian, Barbara. "The Race for Theory." *Feminist Studies* 14.1 (Spring 1988): 67–79.

Civil Rights Congress. *We Charge Genocide: The Historic Petition to the United Nations for Relief from a Crime of the United States Government Against the Negro People.* Edited by William L. Patterson. New York: International Publishers, 1951.

Clark, Kenneth B. *Prejudice and Your Child.* Boston: Beacon Press, 1955.

Clarke, James. *The Lineaments of Wrath: Race, Violent Crime, and American Culture.* New Brunswick: Transaction Publishers, 1998.

Cleaver, Eldridge. *Soul on Ice.* New York: McGraw-Hill, 1968.

Collins, Patricia Hill. *Black Feminist Thought: Knowledge, Consciousness, and the Politics of Empowerment.* New York: Routledge, 1991.

Connerly, Ward. "Where 'Separate but Equal' Still Rules." *New York Times*, May 8, 2000: A23.

Cooley, Thomas. *The Ivory Leg in the Ebony Cabinet: Madness, Race, and Gender in Victorian America.* Amherst: University of Massachusetts Press, 2001.

Cope, Graeme. "'Everybody says all those people . . . were from out of town, but they weren't': A Note on Crowds during the Little Rock Crisis." *Arkansas Historical Quarterly* 67.3 (Autumn 2008): 246–267.

Cresswell, Tim. *In Place/Out of Place: Geography, Ideology, and Transgression.* Minneapolis: University of Minnesota Press, 1996.

———. *Place: A Short Introduction.* Malden, Mass.: Blackwell, 2004.

Works Cited

Crowder, Kyle D. "The Racial Context of White Mobility: An Individual-Level Assessment of the White Flight Hypothesis." *Social Science Research* 29 (2000): 223–257.

Cruea, Susan. "Changing Ideals of Womanhood During the Nineteenth-Century Woman Movement." *American Transcendental Quarterly* 19.3 (2005): 187–204.

Daniel, Pete. *Lost Revolutions: The South in the 1950s.* Chapel Hill: University of North Carolina Press, 2000.

Delaney, David. *Race, Place, and the Law, 1836–1948.* Austin: University of Texas Press, 1998.

Donley, John E. "On Neurasthenia as a Disintegration of Personality." *Journal of Abnormal Psychology* (June 1906): 55–68.

Douglass, Frederick. *The Life and Writings of Frederick Douglass.* Edited by Philip S. Foner. 5 vols. New York: International Publishers, 1950–1975.

———. "The Dred Scott Decision." 1857. In *Life and Writings.* Vol. 2, 407–424.

———. "The Meaning of July Fourth for the Negro." 1852. In *Life and Writings.* Vol. 2, 181–204.

———. *Narrative of the Life of Frederick Douglass: An American Slave.* Edited by David W. Blight. Boston: Bedford/St. Martins, 2003.

———. "The Word 'White.'" 1854. In *Life and Writings.* Vol. 5, 319–320.

Dubek, Laura. "The Social Geography of Race in Hurston's *Seraph on the Suwanee.*" *African American Review* 30.3 (Fall 1996): 341–351.

Du Bois, W. E. B. *Writings.* Compiled by Nathan Huggins. New York: The Library of America, 1986.

———. *Black Reconstruction in America, 1860–1880.* New York: Simon & Schuster, 1935.

———. "Criteria of Negro Art." In *Writings,* 993–1002.

———. *Dusk of Dawn.* In *Writings,* 549–803.

———. "Jefferson Davis as a Representative of Civilization." In *Writings,* 811–814.

———. *The Souls of Black Folk.* In *Writings,* 357–548.

———. "The Souls of White Folk." In *Writings,* 923–938.

duCille, Ann. *The Coupling Convention: Sex, Text, and Tradition in Black Women's Fiction.* New York: Oxford University Press, 1993.

Dwyer, Owen J., and John Paul Jones III. "White Socio-Spatial Epistemology." *Social and Cultural Geography* 1.2 (2000): 209–222.

Dyer, Richard. *White.* New York: Routledge, 1997.

Ellison, Ralph. "Brave Words for a Startling Occasion." In *Shadow and Act,* 102–106. New York: Quality Paperback Book Club, 1953.

———. *Invisible Man.* New York: Vintage Books, 1947.

Ethiop. "What Shall We Do with the White People?" In *Black on White: Black Writers on What It Means to Be White,* 58–66. Edited by David Roediger. New York: Schocken Books, 1998.

Feimster, Crystal. *Southern Horrors: Women and the Politics of Rape and Lynching.* Cambridge: Harvard University Press, 2009.

Works Cited

Fikes, Robert, Jr. "Escaping the Literary Ghetto: African American Authors of White Life Novels, 1946–1994." *Western Journal of Black Studies* 19.2 (1995): 105–112.

———. "How Major Book Review Editors Stereotype Black Authors." *Journal of Blacks in Higher Education* 33 (Autumn 2001): 110–113.

———. "The Persistent Allure of Universality: African-American Authors of White Life Novels, 1845–1945." *Western Journal of Black Studies* 21 (1997): 225–231.

Fishkin, Shelley Fisher. "Desegregating American Literary Studies." In *Aesthetics in a Multicultural Age*, 121–134. Edited by Emory Elliott, Louis Freitas Caton, and Jeffrey Rhyne. New York: Oxford University Press, 2002.

Foster, Gwendolyn Audrey. *Performing Whiteness: Postmodern Re/Constructions in the Cinema.* Albany: State University of New York Press, 2003.

Foucault, Michel. "The Subject and Power." In *Power: The Essential Works of Foucault, 1954–1984.* Vol. 3, 326–348. Edited by James Faubion. Translated by Robert Hurley. New York: The New Press, 2001.

Frankenberg, Ruth. *White Women, Race Matters: The Social Construction of Whiteness.* Minneapolis: University of Minnesota Press, 1993.

Franklin, John Hope. *The Militant South, 1800–1861.* Cambridge: Harvard University Press, 1956.

Freeman, Greg. "Little Rock Central High School National Historic Site." *Encyclopedia of Arkansas History and Culture.* Central Arkansas Library System, last updated January 17, 2012. Website, accessed June 23, 2012.

Gallagher, Charles A., and France Winddance Twine. "The Future of Whiteness: A Map of the 'Third Wave.'" In *Retheorizing Race and Whiteness in the 21st Century: Changes and Challenges*, 1–20. Edited by Charles A. Gallagher and France Winddance Twine. New York: Routledge, 2011.

Gates, Henry Louis, Jr. *Figures in Black: Words, Signs, and the "Racial" Self.* New York: Oxford University Press, 1987.

———. "Mister Jefferson and the Trials of Phillis Wheatley." National Endowment of the Humanities, n.d. Website, accessed July 9, 2012.

Gates, Lorraine. "Power from the Pedestal: The Women's Emergency Committee and the Little Rock School Crisis." *Arkansas Historical Quarterly* 66.2 (Summer 2007): 194–223.

Gearhart, Suzanne. "Foucault's Response to Freud: Sado-Masochism and the Aestheticization of Power." *Style* 29.3 (Fall 1995): 389–403.

Gibbons, William, and Sydney C. Van Nort. "Mamie Phipps Clark: The 'Other Half' of the Kenneth Clark Legacy." *Encounter: Education for Meaning and Social Justice* 22.4 (Winter 2009): 28–32.

Gone with the Wind. Directed by Victor Fleming. MGM, 1939.

Gould, Stephen Jay. *The Mismeasure of Man.* New York: W. W. Norton, 1996.

Graebner, William. *The Age of Doubt: American Thought and Culture in the 1940s.* Boston: Twayne Publishers, 1991.

Works Cited

Graham, Louis. "The White Self-Image Conflict in *Native Son*." *Studies in Black Literature* 3.2 (January 1972): 19–21.

Graham, Maryemma. "Frank Yerby, King of the Costume Novel." *Essence* 6 (October 1975): 70–71, 88–92.

Hale, Grace Elizabeth. *Making Whiteness: The Culture of Segregation in the South, 1890–1940*. New York: Vintage Books, 1998.

Hall, Glinda Fountain. "Inverting the Southern Belle: Romance Writers Redefine Gender Myths." *Journal of Popular Culture* 41.1 (2008): 37–55.

Hall, Jacquelyn Dowd. *Revolt Against Chivalry: Jessie Daniel Ames and the Women's Campaign Against Lynching*. New York: Columbia University Press, 1979.

Harriford, Diane, and Becky Thompson. "Secrets." Civil Rights and Restorative Justice Project. Northeastern University School of Law, November 7, 2010. Website, accessed August 15, 2011.

Harris, Trudier. *Exorcising Blackness: Historical and Literary Lynching and Burning Rituals*. Bloomington: Indiana University Press, 1984.

Hemenway, Robert. *Zora Neale Hurston: A Literary Biography*. Urbana: University of Illinois Press, 1980.

Heneghan, Bridget T. *Whitewashing America: Material Culture and Race in the Antebellum Imagination*. Jackson: University Press of Mississippi, 2003.

Hill, James, L. "The Anti-Heroic Hero in Frank Yerby's Historical Novels." In *Perspectives of Black Popular Culture*, 144–154. Edited by Harry B. Shaw. Bowling Green, Ohio: Bowling Green State University Popular Press, 1990.

Holt, Thomas C. "Marking: Race, Race-Making, and the Writing of History." *American Historical Review* 100.1 (February 1995): 1–20.

hooks, bell. *Black Looks: Race and Representation*. Boston: South End Press, 1992.

———. "Madonna: Plantation Mistress or Soul Sister?" In *Black Looks*, 157–164.

———. "Oppositional Gaze: Black Female Spectators." In *Black Looks*, 115–131.

———. "Representations of Whiteness in the Black Imagination." In *Black Looks*, 165–178.

Horace, Lillian B. *Angie Brown*. Edited by Karen Kossie-Chernyshev. Acton, Mass.: Copley Custom Textbooks, 2008.

———. *The Diary of Lillian B. Horace*. Edited by Karen Kossie-Chernyshev. Boston: Pearson Custom Publishing, 2007.

Horne, Gerald. *Class Struggle in Hollywood, 1930–1950: Moguls, Mobsters, Stars, Reds, and Trade Unionists*. Austin: University of Texas Press, 2001.

Hughes, Langston. "Father and Son." In *The Ways of White Folks*, 207–255. 1933. New York: Vintage Books, 1990.

Hurston, Zora Neale. "The Rise of the Begging Joints." In *Zora Neale Hurston: Folklore, Memoirs, and Other Writings*, 937–944. Compiled by Cheryl A. Wall. New York: The Library of America, 1995.

———. *Seraph on the Suwanee*. 1948. New York: Harper Perennial, 1991.

———. *Their Eyes Were Watching God*. 1937. New York: Harper Perennial, 2006.

———. "What White Publishers Won't Print." In *Zora Neale Hurston: Folklore, Memoirs, and Other Writings*, 950–955. Compiled by Cheryl A. Wall. New York: The Library of America, 1995.

———. *Zora Neale Hurston: A Life in Letters*. Edited by Carla Kaplan. New York: Doubleday, 2002.

Hymowitz, Carol, and Michaele Weissman. *A History of Women in America*. New York: Bantam Books, 1978.

Jackson, Chuck. "Waste and Whiteness: Zora Neale Hurston and the Politics of Eugenics." *African American Review* 34.4 (Winter 2000): 639–660.

Jacobs, Harriet. *Incidents in the Life of a Slave Girl*. 1861. New York: W. W. Norton, 2001.

Jarrett, Gene Andrew, ed. *African American Literature Beyond Race: An Alternative Reader*. New York: New York University Press, 2006.

———. "Frank Yerby." In *African American Literature Beyond Race*, 197–201.

———. "Introduction: 'Not Necessarily Race Matter.'" In *African American Literature Beyond Race*, 1–22.

Jaspin, Elliot. *Buried in the Bitter Waters: The Hidden History of Racial Cleansing in America*. New York: Basic Books, 2007.

Jezebel. Directed by William Wyler. Warner Brother Pictures, 1938.

Johnson, Charles S. *Patterns of Negro Segregation*. New York: Harper & Brothers, 1943.

Johnson, James Weldon. *Along This Way: The Autobiography of James Weldon Johnson*. 1933. New York: Penguin Books, 2008.

Jones, Rhett S. "Nigger and Knowledge: White Double-Consciousness in *Adventures of Huckleberry Finn*." In *Satire or Evasion? Black Perspectives on Huckleberry Finn*, 173–194. Edited by James Leonard, Thomas Tenney, and Thadious Davis. Durham: Duke University Press.

Kelley, William Melvin. *A Different Drummer*. 1959. New York: Anchor Books, 1989.

King, Debra Walker. *African Americans and the Culture of Pain*. Charlottesville: University of Virginia Press, 2008.

King, Martin Luther, Jr. "Eulogy for the Martyred Children." In *I Have a Dream: Writings and Speeches that Changed the World*. Edited by James Melvin Washington. New York: HarperCollins, 1986. 115–118.

———. "Facing the Challenge of a New Age." In *I Have a Dream: Writings and Speeches that Changed the World*. Edited by James Melvin Washington. New York: HarperCollins, 1986. 14–28.

———. "Letter from Birmingham Jail." In *Why We Can't Wait*, 85–112. 1963. New York: Signet Classics, 2000.

Kirk, John A. *Beyond Little Rock: The Origins and Legacies of the Central High Crisis*. Fayetteville: University of Arkansas Press, 2007.

———. *Redefining the Color Line: Black Activism in Little Rock, Arkansas, 1940–1970*. Gainesville: University Press of Florida, 2002.

Works Cited

Klotman, Phyllis R. "A Harrowing Experience: Frank Yerby's First Novel to Film."
CLA Journal 2 (December 31, 1987): 210–222.

Kutchins, Herb, and Stuart A. Kirk. *Making Us Crazy: DSM; The Psychiatric Bible and the Creation of Mental Disorders.* New York: The Free Press, 1997.

Lane, Charles. *The Day Freedom Died: The Colfax Massacre, the Supreme Court, and the Betrayal of Reconstruction.* New York: Henry Holt, 2008.

Lanier, Carlotta Walls. *A Mighty Long Way: My Journey to Justice at Little Rock High School.* New York: One World Trade Paperbacks, 2010.

Lewis, David Levering. *W. E. B. Du Bois: Biography of a Race, 1868–1919.* New York: Henry Holt, 1993.

Lewis, George. *Massive Resistance: The White Response to the Civil Rights Movement.* London: Hodder Education, 2006.

Lewis, John. *Walking with the Wind: A Memoir of the Movement.* San Diego: Harcourt Brace, 1998.

Li, Stephanie. *Something Akin to Freedom: The Choice of Bondage in Narratives by African American Women.* Albany: State University of New York Press, 2010.

Lincoln, C. Eric. *Coming through the Fire: Surviving Race and Place in America.* Durham: Duke University Press, 1996.

Lipsitz, George. *The Possessive Investment in Whiteness.* Philadelphia: Temple University Press, 2006.

Locke, Alain. "Review of *Their Eyes Were Watching God*, by Zora Neale Hurston." 1938. In *Zora Neale Hurston: Critical Perspectives Past and Present*, 18. Edited by Henry Louis Gates Jr. and Kwame Anthony Appiah. New York: Amistad, 1993.

Loewen, James W. *Sundown Towns: A Hidden Dimension of American Racism.* New York: The New Press, 2005.

Long, Richard A. "Creole." In *Harvard Encyclopedia of American Ethnic Groups.* Edited by Stephan Thernstrom. Cambridge: Belknap Press, 1980.

Lott, Eric. "The Whiteness of Film Noir." In *Whiteness: A Critical Reader*, 81–101. Edited by Mike Hill. New York: New York University Press, 1997.

Lutz, Tom. *American Nervousness, 1903: An Anecdotal History.* Ithaca: Cornell University Press, 1991.

Martinot, Steve. *The Machinery of Whiteness: Studies in the Structure of Racialization.* Philadelphia: Temple University Press, 2010.

May, Elaine Tyler. *Homeward Bound: American Families in the Cold War Era.* New York: Basic Books, 1988.

McElrath, Joseph R., Jr., ed. *Critical Essays on Charles W. Chesnutt.* New York: G. K. Hall, 1999.

McElrath, Joseph R., and Robert C. Leitz, eds. *To Be an Author: Letters of Charles W. Chesnutt, 1889–1905.* Princeton: Princeton University Press, 1997.

McKinney, Karyn D. *Being White: Stories of Race and Racism.* New York: Routledge, 2005.

Works Cited

McPherson, Tara. *Reconstructing Dixie: Race, Gender, and Nostalgia in the Imagined South.* Durham: Duke University Press, 2003.

McWilliams, Dean. *Charles W. Chesnutt and the Fictions of Race.* Athens: University of Georgia Press, 2002.

Mills, Charles. *The Racial Contract.* Ithaca: Cornell University Press, 1997.

——. "Racial Exploitation and the Wages of Whiteness." In *What White Looks Like: African American Philosophers on the Whiteness Question*, 25–54. Edited by George Yancy. New York: Routledge, 2004.

Morrison, Toni. *Beloved.* New York: Alfred A. Knopf, 1987.

——. "On the Backs of Blacks." In *The Debate over the Changing Face of America.* Edited by Nicolaus Miller. New York: Touchstone Books, 1994. Reprinted in *What Moves at the Margin: Selected Nonfiction*, 145–148. Edited by Carolyn C. Denard. Jackson: University Press of Mississippi, 2008. Page references are to the 2008 edition.

——. *Playing in the Dark: Whiteness and the Literary Imagination.* New York: Vintage Books, 1992.

Napier, Winston, ed. *African American Literary Theory: A Reader.* New York: New York University Press, 2000.

Nevels, Cynthia. *Lynching to Belong: Claiming Whiteness through Racial Violence.* College Station: Texas A&M University Press, 2007.

Patton, John H. "A Transforming Response: Martin Luther King Jr.'s 'Letter from Birmingham Jail.'" *Rhetoric and Public Affairs* 7.1 (2004): 53–66.

Petry, Ann. *Country Place.* Boston: Houghton Mifflin, 1947.

Phillips, Kimberly L. *War! What Is It Good For? Black Freedom Struggles and the U.S. Military from World War II to Iraq.* Chapel Hill: University of North Carolina Press, 2012.

Plant, Deborah G. *Every Tub Must Sit on Its Own Bottom: The Philosophy and Politics of Zora Neale Hurston.* Urbana: University of Illinois Press, 1995.

Poirier, Suzanne. "The Weir Mitchell Rest Cure: Doctor and Patients." *Women's Studies* 10.1 (January 1983): 15–40.

Powdermaker, Hortense. *After Freedom: A Cultural Study in the Deep South.* Madison: University of Wisconsin Press, 1939.

Rampell, Catherine. "The Help-Wanted Sign Comes with a Frustrating Asterisk." *New York Times*, July 25, 2011.

Reed, Adolph L. *W. E. B. Du Bois and American Political Thought.* New York: Oxford University Press, 1997.

Regester, Charlene. "African-American Writers and Pre-1950 Cinema." *Literature/Film Quarterly* 29.3 (July 2001): 210–235.

Relph, Edward. *Place and Placelessness.* London: Pion Limited, 1976.

Roberts, Terrence. *Lessons from Little Rock.* Little Rock: Butler Center Books, 2009.

Roediger, David, ed. *Black on White: Black Writers on What It Means to Be White.* New York: Schocken Books, 1998.

Works Cited

Rosenberg, Charles E. "The Place of George M. Beard in Nineteenth-Century Psychiatry." *Bulletin of the History of Medicine* 36 (1962): 245–259.

Scharnhorst, Gary. "'The Growth of a Dozen Tendrils': The Polyglot Satire of Chesnutt's *The Colonel's Dream.*" In *Critical Essays on Charles Chesnutt*, 271–280. Edited by Joseph R. McElrath, Jr. New York: G. K. Hall, 1999.

Shapiro, Herbert. *White Violence and Black Response: From Reconstruction to Montgomery.* Amherst: University of Massachusetts Press, 1988.

"Shattered Arcadia, A." Review of *The Colonel's Dream*, by Charles Chesnutt. In *Critical Essays on Charles W. Chesnutt*, p. 92. Edited by Joseph R. McElrath. New York: G. K. Hall, 1999. Reprinted from the *New York Times Saturday Review of Books* 54 (September 16, 1905).

Sibley, David. "Creating Geographies of Difference." In *Human Geography Today*, 115–128. Edited by Doreen Massey, John Allen, and Philip Sarre. Cambridge: Polity Press, 1999.

Smith-Rosenberg, Carroll. *Disorderly Conduct: Visions of Gender in Victorian America.* New York: Oxford University Press, 1986.

Soja, Edward W. *Postmodern Geographies: The Reassertion of Space in Critical Social Theory.* London: Verso, 1989.

Sokol, Jason. *There Goes My Everything: White Southerners in the Age of Civil Rights, 1945–1975.* New York: Alfred A. Knopf, 2006.

St. Clair, Janet. "The Courageous Undertow of Zora Neale Hurston's *Seraph on the Suwanee.*" *Modern Language Quarterly* 50.1 (1989): 38–57.

Sullivan, Shannon. *Revealing Whiteness: The Unconscious Habits of Racial Privilege.* Bloomington: Indiana University Press, 2006.

Tate, Claudia. *Psychoanalysis and Black Novels: Desire and the Protocols of Race.* New York: Oxford University Press, 1998.

Thandeka. *Learning to Be White: Money, Race, and God in America.* New York: Continuum, 1999.

Thomas, Lord Hugh. "Exploring the Spanish Empire." Interview by Robert Siegel. *All Things Considered*, National Public Radio, August 19, 2011. Website, accessed August 19, 2011.

Thomson, Robin J., PA2. "The Coast Guard and the Women's Reserve in World War II." Women in the U.S. Coast Guard, United States Coast Guard Historian's Office, October 1992. Website, accessed September 27, 2012.

Thurman, Howard. *The Luminous Darkness.* New York: Harper & Row, 1965.

Turner, Darwin T. "Frank Yerby as Debunker." *Massachusetts Review* 9.3 (Summer 1968): 569–577.

U.S. National Library of Medicine. "Becoming 'The Father of the Blood Bank,' 1938–1941." Profiles in Science, *The Charles R. Drew Papers.* Website, accessed June 25, 2012.

U.S. Navy. "World War II Era WAVES: Overview and Special Image Selection." *Naval History and Heritage Command.* Website, accessed September 27, 2012.

Works Cited

Walker, Alice. *Sent by Earth: A Message from the Grandmother Spirit*. New York: Seven Stories Press, 2001.

Walker, David. *David Walker's Appeal to the Coloured Citizens of the World*. Edited by Charles M. Wiltse. New York: Hill and Wang, 1965.

Wallace-Sanders, Kimberly. *Mammy: A Century of Race, Gender, and Southern Memory*. Ann Arbor: University of Michigan Press, 2008.

Walsh, Andrea S. *Women's Film and Female Experience, 1940–1950*. New York: Praeger, 1984.

Washington, Mary Helen. "A Woman Half in Shadows." In *Modern Critical Views: Zora Neale Hurston*, 123–138. Edited by Harold Bloom. Philadelphia: Chelsea House, 1986.

Watson, Veronica T. "Lillian B. Horace and the Literature of White Estrangement: Rediscovering an African American Intellectual of the Jim Crow Era." *Mississippi Quarterly* 64.1 (Winter 2011): 3–23.

Wells, Susan. "Discursive Mobility and Double Consciousness in S. Weir Mitchell and W. E. B. Du Bois." *Philosophy and Rhetoric* 35.2 (2002): 120–137.

Wells-Barnett, Ida B. "Lynch Law in America." *The Arena* 23.1 (January 1900): 15–24.

———. "A Red Record." In *On Lynchings*, 55–151. Amherst, N.Y.: Humanity Books, 2002.

———. "Southern Horrors." In *On Lynchings*, 25–54. Amherst, N.Y.: Humanity Books, 2002.

Welter, Barbara. "The Cult of True Womanhood, 1820–1860." *American Quarterly* 18.2 (Summer 1966): 151–174.

West, M. Genevieve. *Zora Neale Hurston and American Literary Culture*. Gainesville: University Press of Florida, 2005.

White, Walter. *Rope and Faggot: A Biography of Judge Lynch*. New York: Alfred A. Knopf, 1929.

Williams, C. Fred. "Class: The Central Issue in the 1957 Little Rock School Crisis." *Arkansas Historical Quarterly* 56.3 (Autumn 1997): 341–344.

Wilson, Matthew. *Whiteness in the Novels of Charles W. Chesnutt*. Jackson: University Press of Mississippi, 2004.

Wilson, William Julius, and Richard P. Taub. *There Goes the Neighborhood: Racial, Ethnic, and Class Tensions in Four Chicago Neighborhoods and Their Meaning for America*. New York: Alfred A. Knopf, 2006.

Wonham, Henry. "Howells, Du Bois, and the Effect of 'Common Sense': Race, Realism, and Nervousness in *An Imperative Duty* and *The Souls of Black Folk*." In *Criticism and the Color Line: Desegregating American Literary Studies*, 126–139. New Brunswick: Rutgers University Press, 1996.

Wray, Matt. *Not Quite White: White Trash and the Boundaries of Whiteness*. Durham: Duke University Press, 2006.

Wright, Richard. "Between Laughter and Tears." Review of *Their Eyes Were Watching God*, by Zora Neale Hurston. *New Masses* 5 (October 1937): 22, 25.

———. *Native Son*. 1940. New York: Harper Perennial, 1993.

Works Cited

X, Malcolm. "The Ballot or the Bullet." In *Malcolm X Speaks: Selected Speeches and Statements*, 23–44. Edited by George Breitman. New York: Grove Weidenfeld, 1965.

———. "God's Judgment of White America." In *The End of White World Supremacy: Four Speeches by Malcolm X*, 121–148. Edited by Benjamin Karim. New York: Arcade Publishing, 1971.

Yancy, George. "Introduction: Fragments of a Social Ontology of Whiteness." In *What White Looks Like: African American Philosophers on the Whiteness Question*, 1–23. Edited by George Yancy. New York: Routledge, 2004.

———. *Look, a White! Philosophical Essays on Whiteness*. Philadelphia: Temple University Press, 2012.

———, ed. *What White Looks Like: African American Philosophers on the Whiteness Question*. New York: Routledge, 2004.

Yerby, Frank. *The Foxes of Harrow*. Garden City, N.Y.: Sun Dial Press, 1946.

———. "How and Why I Write the Costume Novel." *Harper's Magazine* (October 1959): 145–150.

INDEX

Index

CPSIA information can be obtained at www.ICGtesting.com
Printed in the USA
LVOW10s1245130515

438346LV00001B/44/P